Y0-BQW-862

J. M. HODGES LEARNING CENTER
WHARTON COUNTY JUNIOR COLLEGE
WHARTON, TEXAS 77488

Enter, Mysterious Stranger

Enter, Mysterious Stranger

American Cloistral Fiction

by Roy R. Male

University of Oklahoma Press: Norman

Books by Roy R. Male

Hawthorne's Tragic Vision (Austin, 1957)
American Literary Masters (coeditor, New York, 1965)
Types of Short Fiction (editor, Belmont, California, 2d ed., 1970)
Enter, Mysterious Stranger (Norman, 1979)

Library of Congress Cataloging in Publication Data

Male, Roy R.
Enter, mysterious stranger.

Includes bibliographical references and index.
1. American fiction—History and criticism.
2. Outsiders in literature. 3. Community in literature.
4. Fiction—Technique. I. Title.
PS374.094M3 813'.01 79-4736

Manufactured in the U.S.A.
First edition.

To Carolyn, Mary, and Frank

Contents

Acknowledgments

THE AUTHOR of even a short book incurs many obligations. Brief portions of this one have previously appeared in *Criticism* and *Studies in Short Fiction.* I am grateful to the editors of these journals for permission to reprint. The Research Council of the University of Oklahoma provided typing of the manuscript. And I owe more than the footnotes can indicate to the aesthetic theories of Morse Peckham.

My deeper obligations are less formal. In class and out I have been encouraged and enlightened by former students like Pat Anderson, Terry Britton, Jerry Holt, David Russell, Nancy Skinner, and Karen Wells. My colleague Ronald Schleifer offered many valuable suggestions. And I was particularly fortunate to have the research assistance and friendship of Leanne Daggett.

ROY R. MALE

Norman, Oklahoma

There remains in man's sense of achievement the suspicion of its infantile roots; and since his earliest sense of reality was learned by the painful testing of inner and outer goodnesses and badnesses, man remains ready to expect from some enemy, force, or event in the outer world that which, in fact, endangers him from within: from his own split inner world. Thus he is always irrationally ready to fear invasion by vast and vague forces which are other than himself.

Erik Erikson, *Childhood and Society*

Something has to happen in a story, . . . and the simplest thing ever to have happen is to say: Enter, mysterious stranger.

Robert Penn Warren,
"'Blackberry Winter': A Recollection"

Foreword

THIS LITTLE BOOK studies a certain kind of American fiction. No, the book doesn't study it; *I* do. So before I adopt the appropriately detached tone of the literary critic, let me begin on a personal note. I am an English teacher who once, years ago, thought he might become a writer. And I have been fascinated for a long time by the mystery of fiction, how it gets written, what happens when I try to teach it, by the gap between "creative writing" and the academic criticism of literature. More particularly, I have been curious about one kind of story, the story of The Mysterious Stranger. One night, over a decade ago, a version of that story happened in real life. None of us who were there will ever forget it. But I've never been able to write a story about it.

Let me tell you what happened, just laying out the facts. In November, during the mid-1960s, a group of us professors from the University of Oklahoma attended a convention of the South Central Modern Language Association in West Texas. It was a rather dull meeting, and at a publisher's cocktail party some of us decided to join some former graduate students from a Kansas university, take two cars, and go to a night club about thirteen miles out of town. I've forgotten the name of the club, but it was surprisingly congenial, had good food, liquor, and entertainment. About midnight we noticed that one of our group, a Ph.D. candidate named Harry, was getting pretty drunk. It was time to go.

The Kansas bunch invited us to stop in at their motel for a nightcap. They drove off in their Impala, and we followed in our OU station wagon. At the Corral Motel we cracked open the bourbon and scotch, settled in for a final drink, and then somebody said: "Where's Harry?" It turned out that they thought he was in our car; we thought he was in theirs. The fact was that he had been in the men's room, and we'd left him at the night club. Now the question was who would go back thirteen miles in the West Texas darkness and get him.

At that moment there was a banging on the door. We opened it and there stood a gigantic Texan with a bottle of bourbon in one hand and Harry in the other. The Texan was about six and a half feet tall, wore a Stetson and boots, and was furious. We later learned that, a part-owner of the club, he had found Harry, put him in his pickup, and driven him to the motel. As a reward for his trouble, Harry had insulted him all the way, calling him a rustic idiot, someone who would have to study to be a moron, etc. So the Texan greeted us with a remark that still burns in my brain: "You sonsabitches, dipped in degrees. You don't even take care of your own kind."

I knew we were in for it. I had taught out there. I knew how the rich cotton farmers hated the professors, knew that this Texan's name would be Billy Joe or

Bobby Tom or W. J. (Buck) Armistead, knew that he wouldn't leave until he had pushed us around, verbally and maybe physically. Remember he was big. His forearms were the size of my thighs. He could have played tackle for the Dallas Cowboys if he could have understood the signals. And he was saying, "I can buy and sell all of ya." Yet he seemed to want to drink with us and insult us at the same time.

What to do? There were about eleven of us, seven men and four women, I think. But even though some of us had been fairly athletic, had been in the military, we were physically over the hill. Bobby Tom had already picked up the toughest member of our group by the lapels and casually tossed him halfway across the room. And now suddenly he pulled out a knife. So there we were. None of the women present were our wives; we had a university station wagon; I could see the headlines in the local paper the next morning: PROFS ARRESTED IN MOTEL BRAWL.

The first thing we did was assign two men to guard Harry, who was still insulting the Texan but who now started a diatribe about our graduate program. Here was one of our most promising Ph.D. candidates, responding to a specific reality by sharply denouncing Old English verb forms and the experience it had been to study for general exams, etc. (And this was back when Ph.D.s were still getting good jobs.)

Well, I'll cut it short. We did finally persuade Bobby Tom to leave without cutting us to pieces and wrecking the room. And we did finally get Harry to bed. But I remember that night with shame. Seven men afraid of one man. The stereotyped banality of it all, a modern academic version of an episode from "Gunsmoke." The sense of physical impotence weirdly blending with a premonition of impending intellectual sterility. It was the end of something, the end of an era when English professors were high priests presiding over what we thought was a thoroughly functional graduate program.

So much for the actual event. True, it may seem to have been a trivial occurrence, but someone like Joyce Carol Oates could do something with it. How does it get turned into a story? Where to start? Maybe with a description of the setting: "The neon sign of the Corral Motel cut a yellow gash in the black West Texas sky." Too many adjectives, too fancy. Maybe with something more terse, leading directly to the problem we faced. "First rule, familiar to camp counselors and tour guides: always count your people. But we were not camp counselors or tour guides. We were a bunch of English professors and graduate students on our way back from . . ." More promising, but still not quite the right touch. And how much of the story should relate what really happened? How much should be re-created from the distorted dreams I've had of that night ever since? I don't know. That's why I'm an English teacher and not a writer of fiction.

Nevertheless, my abortive efforts at creating a short story convinced me emotionally of some principles I had earlier known from a safe academic distance. They add up to a recognition that fiction, in virtually all its dimensions, is profoundly dual. Writing it, first of all, is an act of self-exposure. The writer learns things about himself and his friends that he ordinarily would prefer to keep hidden. And, as I have indicated, he is likely to reveal his technical shortcomings, his bewilderment about where to cut into the material and shape it in a form that he will not be ashamed of.

But the self-exposure is doubled by a simultaneous act of masking. Even in my brief summary, I concealed Harry's real name, invented some of the dialogue, deliberately avoided naming the college and the town, shielded my colleagues' identity. My claim of "just laying out the facts" was disingenuous; everyone present would have a slightly different version of what really happened.

Enter, Mysterious Stranger

1

Cloistral Fiction

J. HILLIS MILLER says that fiction "is in various ways a chain of displacements—displacement of its author into the invented role of the narrator, further displacement of the narrator into the lives of imaginary characters whose thoughts and feelings are presented in that odd kind of ventriloquism called 'indirect discourse,' displacement of the 'origin' of the story (in historical events or in the life experience of the author) into the fictitious events of the narrative."[1] We might extend Miller's chain to include the displacement of the reader at the moment when he suspends disbelief and allows himself to be carried over the threshold that divides ordinary life from imaginative experience.

That imaginative experience, analyzed formally, is also dual. On the one hand, the story presents itself as a moving stream of impressions—a process; on the other hand, as these impressions succeed one another, they

[1]J. Hillis Miller, "Narrative and History," *Journal of English Literary History* 41 (Fall 1974): 456.

are built into a more or less static structure by the reader.[2] With his customary elegance (and his customary dependence upon skillful manipulation of Greek terms) Northrop Frye designates these two aspects of fictional form as *mythos:* a "secondary imitation of an action," form when it is seen "moving through the work from beginning to end," and *dianoia:* "a secondary imitation of thought," form when it is examined as stationary. The *mythos* "is *dianoia* in movement; the *dianoia* is the *mythos* in stasis."[3]

Even when experienced as process, fiction is not pure movement. The basically temporal character of fictional form is produced by its linguistic medium: as A. A. Mendilow says, "In a novel, what is expressed may in itself be either static and the object of description, or dynamic and the object of narration; in either case, the medium of expression—language—is a process."[4] But language itself possesses a static or spatial dimension, as well as its essentially temporal one, the spatial dimension being its referential aspect. Words are linked with things only by convention or by behavior, but these conventions are as strong as other humanly produced institutions.

Fiction then contains within its own medium the themes of exposure and masking, of movement and

[2]Percy Lubbock, *The Craft of Fiction* (London, 1921), pp. 14–17.

[3]Northrop Frye, *The Anatomy of Criticism* (Princeton, N.J., 1957), p. 83.

[4]A. A. Mendilow, *Time and the Novel* (London, 1952), p. 23. In this paragraph I am also indebted to Joseph Richard Whittington, "The Regional Novel of the South" (Ph.D. diss., University of Oklahoma, 1963), p. 5.

stasis. Like other humanly contrived instruments, it is both a way of knowing and a way of confronting and confessing what cannot be known. As a way of knowing, its traditional subgenres include the quest, the *Bildungsroman,* the efficiently constructed detective story. As a way of confronting the enigmas of human existence, its subgenres include the meaningless journey (*The Narrative of Arthur Gordon Pym, Le Voyage D'Urien*), the dark interiors of the Gothic, and, most specifically, the story of the mysterious stranger.

I propose to test, expand, and qualify these general observations by examining some representative stories in this final category. They are mostly short and mostly American. I have not tried to be exhaustive in examples. Tzvetan Todorov writes that, "Whatever the number of phenomena (of literary works, in this case) studied, we are never justified in extrapolating universal laws from them; it is not the quantity of observations, but the logical coherence of a theory that finally matters."[5] I have included among my examples some plays, since the kind of fiction to be discussed is closely related to drama. Omission of Continental and Oriental narratives results from my own limitations, not from any theoretical principles. I have included some British stories, partly to avoid uttering too many lofty but finally untenable generalization about the uniqueness of American fiction.

The American novel, we have been told by Leslie Fiedler and others, has as its hero a man in motion, as its structure the journey through a dreamlike landscape or

[5]Tzvetan Todorov, *The Fantastic,* trans. Richard Howard (Cleveland, Ohio, 1973), p. 4.

seascape, as its theme the guest for identity. The dissenting voice murmuring, "Ah yes, *Heart of Darkness* by that great American writer, Joseph Conrad," is temporarily stilled as we once again submit to the appeal of the familiar examples: Leatherstocking padding silently through the wilderness, Ishmael and Ahab on the *Pequod* as it plunges off into the lone Atlantic on Christmas Day, Huck and Jim on the raft, Frederick Henry retreating in the rain, Gatsby and Willie Stark spraying gravel as their automobiles hurtle into the night. Bemused by these unforgettable itinerants, we are tempted to say that in its fiction as in its life America is distinguished by the mobility of its individuals.[6]

But just as no one who has driven a car in Europe will find this simple attribution of traits very convincing, so the reader will remember too many non-American traveling heroes and too many nontraveling American heroes to accept the exclusiveness of the above characterization. It is a truism that every supposedly distinctive American trait can be matched by its opposite; we are materialists with a curiously strong streak of idealism, isolationists who have consistently intervened, futurists who bathe in nostalgia, and so on. Over against Whitman's call to the open road that Lawrence found so appealing can be set Emerson's equally eloquent slogan:

[6]See Leslie A. Fiedler, *Love and Death in the American Novel* (New York, 1960), p. xx. Daniel Hoffman, in *Form and Fable in American Fiction* (New York, 1961), p. xiv, says, "The most general statement one might make is that the hero of American folktale, legend, and romance is likely to go on a journey of self-discovery."

"We are built not like a ship to be tossed, but like a house to stand." Thus Richard Chase's characterization of the American novel as being akin to romance and melodrama in its unresolved contradictions seems more valid than Fiedler's.

But, again, as Erik Erikson has pointed out, all national identities are dialectical. Are there not large unresolved contradictions in *Wuthering Heights* and *Vanity Fair?* In short, what makes any given story distinctively American seems to be a much subtler matter of attitude or tone than either of these characterizations can offer. Furthermore, the kinship of such writers as Melville, Conrad, and Faulkner suggests that personal, thematic, generic, and technical considerations may be at least as important as national backgrounds in the study of fiction.

Granting these necessary qualifications, it is probably true that our geography and history have made the choice between mobility and stability more available and thus more intense than it has been for Europeans. The same American child. Erik Erikson points out, may have been exposed in succession or alternately to "sudden decisions expressing the slogans, 'Let's get the hell out of here,' and, 'Let's stay and keep the bastards out.'"[7] If one major strain of American fiction does indeed deal with a person on the run, there is an important minor strain that dramatizes in one form or another the decision to stand firm and confront invasion.

[7]Erik Erikson, *Cildhood and Society,* 2d ed. (New York, 1963), p. 286.

In America the kind of story I have in mind begins with the earliest piece of fiction that can by any stretch of definition be called a short story—Washington Irving's "The Little Man in Black," one of the *Salmagundi* papers (November 24, 1807). The story, narrated by one of Irving's personae, Launcelot Langstaff, tells how the inhabitants of an isolated village react when a mysterious little man moves in among them. Since he always wears black, carries a big book, and never talks except sometimes to himself in an outlandish tongue, the villagers suspect him of witchcraft, and he becomes the bugbear of every house. Pelted and jeered at by the children, gossiped about by the housewives, he finds his only companion in an old dog whose howls finally attract Langstaff's grandfather one night to the stranger's lonely deathbed. Before he dies, the little man reveals that he is the last descendant of Linkum Fidelius, whose sayings provide one of the connecting links among the *Salmagundi* papers.

Irving's ending and his narrative technique deliberately prevent us from taking the story too seriously. Nevertheless, "The Little Man in Black" serves as the American prototype of a large group of stories and plays about the invasion of a town, café, institution, or home by one or more mysterious intruders whose names often provide the title: Hawthorne's "The Gray Champion," Poe's "The Devil in the Belfry," Melville's "The Lightning-Rod Man," Twain's *The Mysterious Stranger,* Hemingway's "The Killers," Faulkner's "Spotted Horses," Malamud's "The Jewbird," Rooney's "Cyclists' Raid." Or the title may contain the name of the place invaded: Harte's "The Luck of Roaring Camp," Crane's "The Blue Hotel," Twain's "The Man That Corrupted Hadleyburg," McCullers's "The Ballad of the Sad Café," Kesey's *One Flew over the Cuckoo's Nest.* Or the title may refer to a season or a symbol: Steinbeck's "The Chrysanthemums," Porter's "Noon Wine," Hemingway's "The Snows of Kilimanjaro," Warren's "Blackberry Winter." Despite their important differences these stories share as their obvious subject the effect of intrusion upon an individual, a family, or a community. Though we can hardly avoid following Mark Twain in calling this kind of fiction the story of the mysterious stranger, it is convenient to have an adjective for it, and as "cloistral," to be complementary to "picaresque."

For the cloistral story is the quest or the picaresque turned inside out ("outside in" would be better), and perhaps if we used this adjective for it, the category of fiction it describes would be more widely recognized. My admittedly limited essay on it published some years ago seems to have disappeared without a ripple into scholarly oblivion.[8] But the category exists for writers, whether or not critics recognize it. As Robert Penn Warren said concerning "Blackberry Winter," "Something has to happen in a story if there is to be more than a dreary lyric poem posing as a story to promote the cause of universal boredom and deliquescent prose. Something had to happen [in my story], and the simplest

[8] Roy R. Male, "The Story of the Mysterious Stranger in American Fiction," *Criticism* 3 (Fall 1961): 281–94.

thing ever to have happen is to say: Enter, mysterious stranger."[9]

The cloistral story follows this typical pattern. Into an isolated setting intrude one or more mysterious strangers who are potential saviors, potential destroyers, or ambiguous combinations of both. There then occurs some form of transaction between the external and the internal, a testing or transformation of the insiders by the intruder(s). The test may be a physical or emotional or rhetorical duel; the transaction is typically a bargaining session of some sort; and the transformation may involve the effort of the insider to break out of his fixed orientation, or it may result in the insider's displacement by the intruder. Then the stranger usually departs—sometimes from this world—leaving the insider(s) to ponder the significance of the experience.

At the risk of arbitrarily separating fictional types that in fact overlap, we need at this point to distinguish the cloistral story from two narrative patterns that are adjacent to it. We exclude from our canon those stories in which the traveling protagonist meets a mysterious stranger. In "Young Goodman Brown," to take one of many examples, the strange devil figure that Brown encounters in the forest (or in his dream of the forest) surely qualifies as mysterious, but he does not intrude upon a fixed setting. The story is thus a variant of the quest and more specifically of the night journey; it is not what we have defined as cloistral fiction. Nor do we

[9]"'Blackberry Winter': A Recollection," in *Understanding Fiction*, ed. Cleanth Brooks and Robert Penn Warren, 2d ed. (New York, 1959)p. 640.

include stories in which the intruder is not, strictly speaking, a stranger. Here the overlapping is extremely close, since the intruder may look unfamiliar to the natives. But if he is a former resident like Rip Van Winkle or Ethan Brand or Hickey in O'Neill's *The Iceman Cometh* or the older son in David Rabe's *Sticks and Bones,* his story might more accurately be called that of the Exile's Return.[10]

To keep our category as "pure" as possible, we must also exclude those narratives in which we eventually take the point of view of the stranger or follow him on his travels. Charles Brockden Brown's *Wieland* looks like a cloistral novel. It portrays the disastrous effect of a seemingly supernatural and certainly ambiguous stranger, Carwin, upon Wieland and his family. Carwin, whose strange power turns out to be ventriloquism, looks just like Melville's lightning-rod man (and a score of other Gothic villains). But later in the book we take his point of view. Without judging the effectiveness of this shift (we are endeavoring to be descriptive, not prescriptive), we can say that it takes *Wieland* off our list. The same point can be made about Faulkner's *Light in August.* The description of Joe Christmas's entrance in chapter 2 fits our category perfectly, but it is part of a larger narrative in which we take his point of view part of the time and travel with him in his quest for identity.

The cloistral story obviously cuts across some categories familiar to those who have wandered in

[10]I have outlined the conventions of this kind of story in "'Babylon Revisited': A Story of the Exile's Return," *Studies in Short Fiction 2* (Spring 1965): 270–77.

bookstores: westerns, gothics, science fiction, mysteries. And it includes poetry ("The Raven," "Flammonde"), as well as drama and fiction. Readers temperamentally averse to classification (more accurately to *new kinds* of classification since we cannot find our way across the street without categorization) may object that the brief scenario supplied above describes *Hamlet, Shane,* a "Gunsmoke" episode called *The Tarnished Badge* and the latest science fiction about invaders from outer space as well as it describes Porter's "Noon Wine," Sherwood's *The Petrified Forest,* and Melville's "Bartleby the Scrivener." Of course it does. Literary classes do not contain built-in evaluation systems. Quests, tragedies, comedies, picaresque novels can be bad or good, crude or slick, tailored either to support or to frustrate the fantasies and expectations of various audiences and readers.

But the great advantage of defining fictions according to the elemental action imitated (as in Lionel Trilling's definition of the story of the Young Man from the Provinces) is that we gain a category that is easily recognizable, distinct without being overly rigid. More subtle categories like point of view do not provide a desirable means for primary classification, that is, for discovering fundamental similarities. Henry James wrote that "the execution belongs to the author alone: it is what is most personal to him, and we measure him by that."[11] To classify according to technique, then, pigeonholes an author where he most justly claims his uniqueness. Our first aim, to quote James again and in a slightly different

[11]Henry James, "The Art of Fiction," *Partial Portraits* (London, 1888), p. 385.

connection, is to "get the correspondences and equivalents that make differences mean something."[12] We proceed then to the main "correspondences and equivalents," the major conventions of this kind of story.

[12]Henry James, *The Art of the Novel,* ed. R. P. Blackmur (New York, 1934), p. 132.

2

The Conventions

ONE MAJOR AND OBVIOUS convention of cloistral fiction is its isolated, circumscribed setting. Reflecting its origins in drama, all or nearly all of the action occurs in one place. New characters are introduced as if they were entering a stage, and movement is limited. The setting may not be actually fixed—it may be a floating ship, for instance—but it is enclosed. In short, for an intruder to be perceived as incongruous, for the threat of displacement to occur, there must be established a prior sense of regional, institutional, or domestic identity.

In a play this atmosphere is accomplished by the set, stage directions, and dialogue. But in extending this sense backward in time, the teller of tales has a considerable advantage over the playwright, an advantage that was probably underrated before Wayne Booth showed how critics had overemphasized the dramatic element in fiction.[1] Interesting as it is, George Bluestone's movie of "Bartleby" could not capture the delightfully insane

[1]Wayne Booth, *The Rhetoric of Fiction* (Chicago, 1961).

routine of the law office, nor could the televised version of "Noon Wine" reproduce the gradual disintegration of Mr. Thompson's farm:

God amighty, it did look like somebody around the place might take a rake in hand now and then and clear up the clutter around the barn and the kitchen steps. The wagon shed was so full of broken-down machinery and ragged harness and old wagon wheels and battered milk pails and rotting lumber you could hardly drive in there any more. Not a soul on the place would raise a hand to it, and as for him, he had all he could do with his regular work. He would sometimes in the slack season sit for hours worrying about it, squirting tobacco on the ragweeds growing in a thicket against the woodpile, wondering what a fellow could do, handicapped as he was.

It is no accident, therefore, that many stories of this kind are written from the perspective of a region's "oldest inhabitant," a narrative voice like the one Stephen Vincent Benét experimented with before he wrote "The Devil and Dan'l Webster." So stories like "The Gray Champion," Hardy's "The Three Strangers," and "The Ballad of the Sad Café" are told by narrators who seem omniscient about the deeply rooted customs of their region. Even a play like Arthur Miller's *A View from the Bridge* uses Alfieri, a lawyer, as a kind of stage manager–narrator who speaks directly to the audience:

I am inclined to notice the ruins in things, perhaps because I was born in Italy. . . . I only came here when I was twenty-five. In those days, Al Capone, the greatest Carthaginian of all, was learning his trade on these pavements, and Frankie Yale himself was cut precisely in half by a machine gun on the corner of Union Street, two blocks away. Oh, there were many here who were justly shot by unjust men. Justice is very important here.

The amount of historical depth attributed to the setting varies, of course, from the richly detailed folk customs of "The Three Strangers" to the straight history at the beginning of "The Gray Champion" to the almost purely dramatic technique of "The Killers." Hardy's rather inept effort to dramatize his successful short story in a play called *The Three Wayfarers* illustrates the point exactly. He is unable to realize his description of the setting; he omits the location of the shepherd's house—a crossroads in the midst of a desolate area—which is crucial, both for the probability of three strangers stopping at the same house and for the story's symbolic richness. "At the crossroads contraries intersect: birth and death, freedom and captivity, boldness and timidity, natural violence and rural domesticity, justice and law."[2]

The famous dramatic technique of "The Killers" can ultimately be justified, but the setting of the story does raise some nagging questions about its realism. Hemingway's refusal to fill in the past leaves us with the feeling that Summit, the town where the action occurs, is "flat." Though it is supposedly a small town, the inhabi-

[2]Alexander Fischler, "Theatrical Techniques in Thomas Hardy's Short Stories," *Studies in Short Fiction* 3 (Summer 1966): 443. On the motif of the Mysterious Stranger in Hardy's fiction see J. O. Bailey, "Hardy's 'Mephistophelian Visitants,'" *Publications of the Modern Language Association* 61 (December 1946): 1146–81; and Albert J. Guérard, *Thomas Hardy: The Novels and Stories* (Cambridge, Mass., 1949), pp. 96–99.

tants seem hardly to know one another. After the killers have gone, why doesn't Nick or George report to the chief of police? Why, when they leave, do the killers appear completely unconcerned about this possibility? We last see them walking across the street. No car. Where are they going and how?

As Edward Stone has indicated, these and other questions are at least partly answered when we realize that the actual model for Henry's restaurant was a place called Kitsos, situated not in Summit but in Chicago. Hemingway told Gene Tunney that the fictional Ole Andreson was Carl Andreson, and the town was Summit, Illinois. "But that's all I told him because the Chicago mob that sent the killers was, and, as, far as I know, is still very much in business. . . . I guess I left as much out of 'The Killers' as any story I ever wrote. Left out the whole city of Chicago." As Stone says, the story as Hemingway chose to write it "does have a flavor that relocating it (leaving it, more precisely) in Chicago might mar: the stage is small, the cast is intimate, and there is a correspondingly effective intimacy to the horror of the story that might have been difficult to bring off in a big-city restaurant. It is also true that the undefinable quality of suggested foreign evil is possible only if the evil *is* foreign to Summit,—only if it comes *from* Chicago rather than being shown in operation there."[3]

Whatever their method—description, summary narrative, cross-talk among characters in a café, stage directions—authors of cloistral stories are intent upon establishing time and place, as their opening sentences

[3]Edward Stone, "Some Questions About Hemingway's 'The Killers,'" *Studies in Short Fiction* 5 (Fall 1967): 15.

indicate: "It was many years ago. Hadleyburg was the most honest and upright town in all the region round about" (Twain). "It was getting into June and past eight in the morning, but there was a fire—even if it wasn't a big fire—just a fire of chunks—on the hearth of the big stone fireplace in the living room" (Warren). "Time: 1896–1905. Place: Small South Texas Farm" (Porter). "It was in 1590—winter. Austria was far away from the world, and asleep; it was still the Middle Ages in Austria, and promised to remain so forever" (Twain).

The settings are thus isolated in place or time or both. And they are circumscribed; one is reminded of Poe's comment in "The Philosophy of Composition" about the locale of "The Raven": "a close circumscription of space is absolutely necessary to the effect of insulated incident," and his further warning that this "must not be confused with mere unity of place." The typical beginning of cloistral stories establishes a feeling of either claustrophobia or its opposite, claustrophilia. Carson McCullers begins "The Ballad of the Sad Café" by presenting the suffocating boredom of life in a small town hermetically sealed off against novelty. *One Flew over the Cuckoo's Nest* plunges us into the caged atmosphere of an institution dominated by Big Nurse. Other stories, like Hawthorne's "The Ambitious Guest" and Warren's "Blackberry Winter," begin with a mood of claustrophilia, the deeply satisfying sense of security and energy conservation produced by the knowledge that one belongs to a cloister or a fireside circle.

With the entrance of the stranger the mythic impinges upon the normal human world. Because they are merely incidents in a larger narrative, the ancient myths are not stories of the mysterious intruder as we have defined them. But they supply the archetypal figures—Christ, Jove, Satan, Mephistopheles, the Shadow, Trickster, Death—that haunt the more modern stories of this kind. In the ancient myths we usually follow the traveling gods and see from more or less an omniscient point of view; to do so in cloistral fiction would be to destroy the possibility of presenting their mystery and slightly supernatural quality. "Certain characters gain in importance and magnetism by being only *seen,*" writes Elizabeth Bowen; "this makes them more romantic, fatal-seeming, sinister. In fact, no character in which these qualities are, for the plot, essential, should be allowed to enter the seeing class."[4] One might add the obvious but important point, to be developed later, that, because we know much more about characters in fiction than we do about living people, the mystery of a stranger in fiction is more tantalizing than it is in life.

All mysterious strangers are by definition incongruous in the local setting. They may be subhuman: a raven, a Jewbird, a hyena, a giant insect; or they may be superhuman: Christ, the Devil, the Angel of the Odd, a ghost, Death, Mephistopheles. In more realistic stories the stranger is simply incongruous in this time or place—A Swede in South Texas or Fort Romper, Nebraska, a city man looking for work on a farm, a baby in Roaring Camp. As Seth says of the stranger in "Blackberry Winter," "There was no place for him to

[4]Elizabeth Bowen, "Notes on Writing a Novel," in *Collected Impressions* (New York, 1950), p. 260.

have come from, and there was no reason for him to come where he was coming, toward our house."

Though there is no logical reason for the entrance of the stranger, it is equally true that he comes as if in answer to some unuttered call. The Gray Champion appears in hours of "darkness, and adversity, and peril"; Eseldorf deserves and in a sense demands Satan as smug Hadleyburg asks for the man to corrupt it; Mr. Helton arrives at the Thompson farm walking "as if he knew the place well and knew where he was going and what he would find there." This is probably a fictional way of saying that mysterious intruders tend to be representative of what man has become alienated from: God, the past, nature, other people, himself. Thus they are almost always potential saviors, destroyers, or ambiguous combinations of both, and their initial entrance, however much it may be displaced toward realism, amounts to the entrance of God or the devil on a machine.

The stranger's mythic dimension makes his departure more difficult for the author than his entrance. He must be disposed of in some way that is both credible and relevant to the theme. The difficulty of managing this exit is suggested by the violent or abrupt or cryptic endings in most of our stories. Warren says, "when I had finished the next to last paragraph I still did not know what to do with my tramp," and it is a safe guess that many of our other authors were in a somewhat similar predicament. The Gray Champion simply fades away, the abruptness of his disappearance softened somewhat by Hawthorne's characteristic device, ambiguity. Harte disposes of the Luck by drowning him in a flood. Clutched by the dying Kentuck, he drifts "away into the shadowy river that flows forever into the unknown sea." *The Confidence-Man* ends with the cosmopolitan "kindly" leading the miserly old man away, presumably to rob him. Melville's last sentence remains enigmatic. It reads, "Something further may follow of this Masquerade," and no one can be quite sure whether he intended a sequel or some secret irony or simply could not find a better ending. Twain solves the difficulty in *The Mysterious Stranger* by having the world disappear along with Satan.

As a fictional character the stranger may or may not be important. In "The Man That Corrupted Hadleyburg" he is a mere shadow; in two Hawthorne stories, "The Gray Champion" and "The Ambitious Guest," he is the central figure. What counts is his effect upon others. Some strangers are simple saints or saviors. The Gray Champion is the "type of New England's hereditary spirit" who transforms the mob to a potentially armed force "ready to convert the very stones of the street into deadly weapons" against tyranny. The Luck, though merely a passive infant and the child of a slut, radically changes the lives of those around him. The supposedly tough inhabitants of Roaring Camp become physically, linguistically, and morally clean, and a vague idea that this is "pastoral happiness" pervades the camp. Mr. Homos, the traveler from Altruria in Howells' novel, stands out from the crowd as a kind of homespun philosopher-king, serene in his simple collective Christian virtues. He inspires the "lower classes" and radically tests the capitalistic assumptions of the elite.

Other strangers are clearly rogues or destroyers: the killers in Hemingway's story, Melville's lightning-rod man, the Red Death in "The Masque of the Red Death,"

Duke Mantee in Sherwood's *The Petrified Forest.* In the more complex stories the intruders are usually dual. Philip Traum, like his illustrious uncle, is an angel but also Satan; the Confidence-man has attributes of both Christ and Satan. Kesey's Randle Patrick McMurphy is a con artist, but he restores manhood to some of the inmates in the asylum. Sometimes the intruder's ambiguity is split into two or more characters. In "Noon Wine" one stranger is a crazy savior, the other a rational devil. Mr. Helton, the lunatic murderer, reminds Mrs. Thompson of a "disembodied spirit," and in the scene where she invites him to go to church with the family he is a menacing figure as he glares at her and lifts his pitchfork. But he saves the farm; he becomes the "hope and prop of the family," while the bounty hunter Hatch, who has the law behind him, could hardly be more repulsive.

The stranger may affect a crowd, a family, or an individual. In the stories involving a crowd, the people normally function as a chorus, reflecting the buzz and hum of their region by a series of clipped colloquial comments. Here, for example, is Harte's crowd, talking about the Luck: "Is that him?" "Mighty small specimen"; "Hasn't more'n got the color"; "Aint bigger nor a derringer." And here is Melville's crowd, whispering about the man who is, "in the extremest sense of the word, a stranger": "Odd fish!" "Poor fellow!" "Who can he be?" "Casper Hauser." "Bless my soul!" "Uncommon countenance." "Green prophet from Utah." "Humbug!" "Singular innocence." "Means something." "Spirit rapper." "Moon-calf."

The crowd may be separated into types, named usually by their occupations. Thus we have the banker—

called Mr. Bullion by Howells and Mr. Pinkerton by Twain—the merchant, the novelist, the tanner, the saddler, the professor, and so on. Or the flat characters are distinguished by the time-honored technique of a recurrent gesture or refrain. Kentuck, in Harte's story, is somewhat overly fond of saying "the d——d little cuss"; the professor in *A Traveller from Altruria* tirelessly noses out the sources of Mr. Homos's utopia, Martini in *One Flew over the Cuckoo's Nest* is remembered by his gifted hallucinations. Little or no effort is made to individualize these types, since the center of interest here is simply the effect of the stranger on the crowd.

Among the insiders we usually find one or more authority figures—a king, a father, a Big Nurse—whose power is most directly challenged by the intruder. The authority may be benign, as in "Blackberry Winter," malignant, a Tyrant Within, as in "The Gray Champion," or a complex figure combining efficiency and treachery (Claudius comes to mind as a prototype here: courteous, efficient, cool in the face of danger but ultimately overweening, self-deceptive, and mean). If an authority is not present, this vacuum automatically becomes part of the problem. "Who's in charge? Why doesn't somebody *do* something?" The ending of "The Blue Hotel" typifies this situation. The cowboy says, "'Well, I didn't do anything, did I?'" And the easterner says that all of them were collaborators in the murder of the Swede. Both are right. All five men collaborated in the crime, yet none of them really controlled the situation.

The most fully developed character in most of these stories is a receptive intelligence, or "receptor," who mediates between the stranger and the crowd or else receives alone the full impact of the intrusion. He may be the narrator and authority figure like the lawyer in "Bartleby" or a mind that the author enters and leaves at will. The stranger affects him more directly than he does the rest of the people and may test the strength of his ties to his family or his community. There may be a pair of receptors like the Thompsons in "Noon Wine" or Mrs. Shortley and Mrs. McIntyre in O'Connor's "The Displaced Person." Obviously the use of such a character adds immediacy, a point to which we shall return when we discuss the relation between the author and the reader in these stories.

At the heart of the cloistral story is the test or transaction or transformation. It is not the intruder himself who is important; it is not the consequence of his coming that is alone of primary importance; rather it is the interaction of insider and outsider that provides the basis for a story and is emphasized in the narrative recounting of the event. This interaction is what makes each story finally unique; each artist's vision leads him to see the confrontation in a different way and to develop it as he envisions it proceeding. In a sense, then, all cloistral stories are a series of footnotes to Ovid's *Metamorphoses,* the poem whose significance finally lies in a theme that widens "to embrace the doctrine that all things are in flux. . . . the metamorphoses as described take place so fluently as to suggest that the identity of species is less hard and fast than we think."[5]

Change, of course, is inherent in all fiction. But by isolating cloistral fiction from other kinds of stories, we can specify and highlight the process. It would be possible to arrange our stories on a scale representing dif-

[5]L. P. Wilkinson, *Ovid Recalled* (Cambridge, Mass., 1955), p. 218.

ferent degrees of transformation, ranging from highly successful to abortive. Thus there are successful metamorphoses in Conrad's *The Secret Sharer,* as the young captain affirms that "no one in the world would stand now between us, throwing a shadow on the way of silent knowledge and mute affection, the perfect communion of a seaman with his first command"; in Dicken's "A Christmas Carol" and "The Haunted Man," as Scrooge and Redlaw affirm belief in human compassion and love; in "The Luck of Roaring Camp," as the miners are transformed into good men, loving, tender, gentle with the child; in "The Gray Champion," as the crowd gains courage from the appearance of a hero; in *One Flew over the Cuckoo's Nest,* as many of the inmates finally learn to cope with the Combine, at least to the extent of going out to face it. This pattern of the affirmative metamorphosis is associated, as we indicated earlier, with the stranger as a savior.

At the other pole is the unsuccessful or abortive transformation, in which the stranger is usually sinister: in "Noon Wine," which ends with the suicide of Mr. Thompson because he does not understand what has happened to him; in "The Devil in the Belfry," which portrays the chaos effected by the intruder upon the once excessively ordered village of Vondervotteimittiss; in all four of Flannery O'Connor's cloistral stories, dealing with people incapable of coping with their handicaps in a positive or useful way; in Cozzens's *S.S. San Pedro,* whose passengers and crew fear death (Dr. Percival) and fail to weather a crisis because no one takes on the authority held by the dying captain.

Ranging in between are those stories in which it is difficult to assess the success or failure of the metamorphosis. Examples are "The Killers," in which Hemingway leaves us in doubt concerning what Nick Adams will really do, and "Bartleby," in which the narrator weakly generalizes about humanity but shows only a slight gain in awareness from the disruptive influence of Bartleby. There are also problem stories like "Blackberry Winter," in which the metamorphosis is complete ("I did follow him, all the years"), but which bring affirmation of misery or of the existence of evil; most of the Poe stories belong in this category. But whatever problems arise in determining the relative success or failure of the transformation, they do address the central question of the story. No matter what opportunity is rejected, what advantage not taken, the final situation is different from the initial one. The stranger may change; the receptor may change; they both may change. But obviously the intrusion of the stranger creates a tension that has to be resolved by some degree of interaction.[6]

This interaction is often objectified in the stories by a minor motif that we may call the break-out: the attempt of the insider to emerge, at least temporarily, from his fixed orientation. Hamlet goes to England, the inmates of Kesey's asylum go on a fishing trip, Nick Adams leaves the lunchroom to see Ole Andreson, Theodore Fischer makes a visionary excursion with Satan. In short, the format of the cloistral story is one way of dramatizing the collapse of assumed Cartesian barriers between subject and object. The external, the strange, does not exist apart from the perceiving self, nor does that self exist in isolation from the world.

[6]I am indebted to an unpublished paper by Karen Wells for part of this summary.

The devil you know is better than the devil you don't.

Old saying

3

Knowing the Unknowable

THE TYPICAL CLOISTRAL STORY, as we have seen, presents us with a model of ordinary waking consciousness deeply imbedded in its routinized psychological, social, and metaphysical assumptions and now suddenly confronted with a problem in the guise of a mysterious intruder. What has been taken for granted as reality is challenged, the precariousness of human identity is laid bare, the mystery of how we interact with the world and with other human beings is concretely dramatized. Our stories, of course, have no monopoly on these classic fictional themes, but the action imitated in cloistral fiction generates them in an intense and simplified way that is convenient for study.

The stranger in Flannery O'Connor's "The Life You Save May Be Your Own" sets forth the basic situation: "I can tell you my name is Tom T. Shiftlet and I come from Tarwater, Tennessee," he says to Mrs. Crater, "but you never seen me before: how you know I ain't lying? How you know my name ain't Aaron Sparks, lady, and I come from Singleberry, Georgia, or how you know it's not George Speeds and I come from Lucy, Alabama, or how you know I ain't Thompson Bright from Toolafalls, Mississippi?" This illuminating (Sparks, Lucy, Bright) diatribe prompts the old woman's sullen rejoinder: "I don't know nothing about you." She (and the reader) face the most obvious and profound problem inherent in cloistral fiction—man's curiosity set over against the limits of rational human knowledge. As Shiftlet goes on to say, ominously: "Maybe the best I can tell you is, I'm a man; but listen, lady, . . . what is a man?"

What is a man? Or, more broadly, what is the strange object that has invaded our consciousness? As a townsman says at the beginning of Faulkner's "Spotted Horses," "What the hell is that?" The problem of how we know what we know begins with the way in which our senses receive and process information. We now know with some degree of measurability what earlier writers have always intuited—that our senses screen out large masses of data to enable us to find our way around in the world and survive. Robert Ornstein's brilliantly persuasive book *The Psychology of Consciousness* indicates the scientific limits of our vision: "In physical fact, the only difference between 'visible light' and the nearby portions of the electromagnetic spectrum is in wavelength. Nothing sacred occurs in nature between the electromagnetic wavelengths of 390 and 400 billionths of a meter, yet we can perceive one and not the other. It is only the receptive characteristics of our eye which give a special place to a wavelength of 400 billionths of a meter, but not to one 390."[1] The monk in Maupassant's "Le

[1] Robert Ornstein, *The Psychology of Consciousness* (New York, 1972), p. 44.

Horla," who may be a philosopher or a fool, puts the enigma more eloquently: "Do we see the hundred-thousandth part of what exists? Look here; there is the wind, which is the strongest force in nature. It knocks down men, and blows down buildings, uproots trees, raises the sea into mountains of water, destroys cliffs and casts great ships onto the breakers; it kills, it whistles, it sighs, it roars. But have you ever seen it, and can you see it? Yet it exists for all that." Hence the intrusion of a being, who, though invisible, nevertheless seems to exist, as in O'Brien's "What Was It?" and "Le Horla," potentially conveys an awesome sense of power.

Sight gives us relatively crude data concerning time (home movie screens reflecting only twenty four discrete flashes of light per second are seen as a continuous picture). In spite of the limitations indicated above, sight offers relatively sensitive data concerning space. And it is directed, the result of some conscious choice to face a certain way and open or close our eyes. Hearing, on the other hand, gives us very crude data concerning space ("Where did that sound come from?") and relatively sensitive temporal data, and, as any victim of sonic booms or the banshee feedback screech of amplifiers can testify, it is difficult to tune out. Thus the mystery of intrusion is often first conveyed by sound—rapping, rustling, clumping footsteps, the key fumbling at a lock. Chief Bromden, the supposedly deaf-and-dumb Indian who narrates *One Flew over the Cuckoo's Nest,* first becomes aware of the intruder McMurphy when "the lockworks rattle strange; it's not a regular visitor at the door. . . . even though I can't see him, I know he's no ordinary Admission." In "Cyclists' Raid," Joel Bleeker hears the roar of the motorcycles before he sees them.

The limitations of our ordinary waking consciousness are culturally as well as neurologically determined. As Ornstein has shown, the left hemisphere of the brain, usually called the "major" hemisphere by Western psychologists and neurologists, is primarily specialized to produce an analytical consciousness. It is object-centered, involving separation of oneself from other objects and organisms. It helps provide "a relatively stable personal world in which we can differentiate objects and act upon them. The concepts of causality, linear time, and language are the essence of this mode." The right, or "minor," hemisphere—minor because the major mode in our culture is verbal and intellectual—is "more holistic and relational, and more simultaneous in its mode of operation."[2] It finds expression in the traditional esoteric psychologies of the East in which Being is an invisible but all-pervasive presence that cannot be captured by analysis. It is, like Melville's shape-shifting Confidence-Man, the stranger "from the East."

Though our senses are sieves whose holes are to some extent culturally determined, the receptors in our stories and we as human beings must respond to intrusive stimuli if we are to survive. More accurately, we exist in a precarious neurological continuum: at one pole, an effort to seal out all stimuli (which leads to insanity and extinction); at the other, a total openness to stimuli (which leads to insanity and extinction). Between the two extremes lie the various intrusions that can be integrated into the reality of ordinary life with a resultant enrichment of it.

[2]Ibid., pp. 52, 64, 184.

Poe is the writer of both extremes: at one end Prince Prospero and his doomed frenetic effort to seal himself and his courtiers off from the Red Death; at the other, Roderick Usher and his morbidly acute senses or the psychotic narrator of "Berenice" with his inability to screen out irrelevant sense data. Poe virtually leaves out the middle; for him, social concerns are almost nonexistent. He pares them away to concentrate on the ways in which "irrational forces and inexplicable phenomena threaten "the monarch of Thought's dominion."[3] In his cloistral fiction the intruders are usually representatives of death, the alter ego, or the devil: the spectral image in "The Masque of the Red Death", the Shadow in the parable of that name, the Angel of the Odd, the devil in the belfry.

In some of these stories the significant question is whether the strange has actually intruded or whether the narrator, because of his mood, has projected the strange upon the familiar. The clearest illustration of this process is Poe's relatively unfamiliar story entitled "The Sphinx." During the dread reign of cholera in New York the narrator is visiting a relative in his cottage on the Hudson. All around them are the ordinary means of summer amusement"—boating, fishing, sketching, bathing—but the constant news of death from the city has changed what might have been a pleasant vacation into a nightmare. "At length," says the narrator, "we

[3]J. Gerald Kennedy, "The Limits of Reason: Poe's Deluded Detectives," *American Literature* 47 (May 1975): 185. See also Robert Shulman, "Poe and the Powers of the Mind," *Journal of English Literary History* 37 (June 1970): 245–62.

trembled at the approach of every messenger. The very air from the South seemed to us redolent with death. That palsying thought, indeed, took entire possession of my soul."

While thus obsessed with omens of death, the narrator sees or thinks he sees a gigantic monster with a death's head on its breast descending a bare hill across the river. His host, looking in the same general direction but from a different seat, sees nothing, and the narrator, overcome by terror, is forced to consider the vision either as an omen of his death or as a sign of paranoiac delusion. Then this riddle of "The Sphinx" is solved by the calm and rather unlikely analysis of the host. An insect called the Death's-headed Sphinx, about one-sixteenth inch long, has been climbing up and down a spider's thread about one-sixteenth inch from the narrator's eye. Because of his obsession with death ordinary laws of perspective have been suspended, and he has projected his distorted image of the tiny insect against the Palisades.

One factor, then, that makes all knowledge uncertain and in more extreme situations mysterious is that mood affects perception. As Paul Brodtkorb puts it, introducing his phenomenological analysis of *Ishmael's White World:* "What it is that lies within 'situation,' determines its personal meaning and explains different apprehensions of similar experience by the same consciousness may be called for want of a better term, *mood.*"[4] And

[4]Paul Brodtkorb, *Ishmael's White World* (New Haven, Conn., 1965), p. 13.

because Poe usually deals with man in extreme situations, doing so with appropriately unsettling prose styles, he remains a deeply discomfiting writer.

So it is something of a relief to move to the ways in which other writers of cloistral fiction handle intruders who appear in some kind of social context. After Poe, we can appreciate Irving's characteristically light touch in "The Stout Gentleman," a parody of all those anecdotes about mysterious personages like the "Wandering Jew, the Man with the Iron Mask . . . The Invisible Girl, and last, though not least, the Pig-Faced Lady." The tale's epigraph—"I'll cross it, though it blast me" (which reminds us, incidentally, that *Hamlet* is one of the archetypal Mysterious Stranger stories)—introduces a sketch in which the narrator spends a rainy November Sunday in an inn in Derby trying to figure out the identity of a nameless traveler. Anticipating *The Confidence-Man,* Irving's narrator notes that with transients "the color of a coat, the shape or size of the person, is enough to suggest a travelling name. It is either the tall gentleman, or the short gentleman, or the gentleman in black, or the gentleman in snuff-color; or, as in the present instance, the stout gentleman. A designation of the kind once hit upon, answers every purpose, and saves all further inquiry." Saves all further inquiry for landlords, perhaps, but not for the curious narrator. From bits and pieces of vague information he constructs various hypotheses about the mysteriously secluded stranger. "What could be the meaning of this solitude and mystery?" he asks himself. "God knows" said I, at my wit's end; 'it may be one of the royal family for aught

I know, for they are all stout gentlemen." The narrator's curiosity *is* the story; the mysterious stranger's importance is summed up in the last line. Scrambling to the window, the narrator finally catches a glimpse of the stout gentleman as he enters a stagecoach. "The skirts of a brown coat parted behind, and gave me a full view of the broad disk of a pair of drab breeches." Irving's point in this parody is the one made more ponderously in Berger and Luckmann's *The Social Construction of Reality*—that we apprehend unknown others "in a continuum of typifications, which are progressively anonymous as they are removed from the 'here and now' of the face-to-face situation."[5] The conclusion of the story presents us with a "face-to-cheek" situation, and thus the stout gentleman remains anonymous.

In *The Confidence-Man* the same practice of identifying transients by labels, external characteristics, and temporary states is followed. But Melville's icy exemplification of his central theme—that reality is inscrutable—exposes the reader to the full range of his epistemological uncertainty. In the first place, the world evoked in the book is radically enclosed and unstable. We are asked to place our faith in the *Fidèle,* a riverboat floating down the Mississippi. But the boat does not seem to have a pilot, and though it stops at various places, it does not really seem to move. Newton Arvin has complained that "there is an infinitely stronger sense of flow and movement in two pages of *Life on the*

[5]Peter Berger and Thomas Luckmann, *The Social Construction of Reality* (New York, 1966), p. 33.

Mississippi than in all the forty-five chapters of Melville's book."[6]

In this unstable and limited world we are confronted not only with the bewildering metamorphoses of the Confidence-Man but also with other unexplained and abrupt changes of shape and identity. In chapter 6 the one-legged cynic is suddenly called the "one-eyed man." Is this an error by Melville or one more transformation? We have no way of knowing. Later in the book (chapter 30) Charlie and Frank seem to have changed identities. Another Melvillean slip? Probably. But it appears in both the first American and the first English editions. What is an editor to do?[7]

Even more unsettling than the slippery spatial outlines represented in the book is the lack of temporal and mnemonic perspective. The reader can handle the fact that all the action occurs on April Fool's Day, for the human beings on board this ship of fools are more representative on that day than they are on the other 364. But the radically discontinuous structure of the book makes its details extremely difficult to remember (imagine the embarrassment of constructing or taking an "objective test" covering *The Confidence-Man*). Richard

[6]Newton Arvin, *Herman Melville* (New York, 1950), pp. 249–50. My response to Arvin's criticism is that *The Confidence-Man* is a cloistral story, not a quest or a picaresque novel. Its structure is enclosed; the rogue is seen from inside a fixed setting, and he makes his entrances and exits in various guises the way the stranger does in "The Man That Corrupted Hadleyburg." We should not confuse this with the structure of the picaresque novel, where we follow the rogue from place to place.

[7]Leon Howard in 1951 pointed out the confusion between Frank

Chase has remarked that continuity is of the essence in the traditional novel. In this antinovel perhaps the most ominous action is that of the lamblike stranger in the first chapter who writes inscriptions about charity upon his slate and then immediately erases them. So the reader with no central character to identify with, no coherent dramatic action, and no consistent perspective finds himself in a position like that of Mr. Roberts in chapter 4; he has a "faithless memory"; the past is "quite erased from the tablet."

The book bristles with references to "real" people and places, contains caricatures and distortions of writers like Emerson and Poe, unashamedly feeds off sources like Judge Hall's *Sketches of History, Life, and Manners in the West.* But Melville insistently reminds us that there is no necessary connection between language and the world: all words are potentially as slippery and ambiguous as the word "confidence." Language, as people are continually discovering and rediscovering, is categorial; even proper names like Ringman, Truman, and Charles Arnold Noble merely ascribe certain attributes to a certain range of experiences.[8] In short. what is being tested by the central device in the first part of the book and what underlies the lengthy conversation between Frank and Charlie in the second part is the "doctrine of labels"

---

and Charlie, and Hershel Parker corrects it in his edition of *The Confidence-Man* (New York, 1971), p. 152. But, as far as I know, no one has noticed that the cynic shifts from having one leg to having one eye.

[8]Morse Peckham, *The Triumph of Romanticism* (Columbia, S.C., 1970), pp. 293–95.

(chapter 36). We say, somewhat too confidently, that "The Confidence Man appears in eight progressive incarnations": the cream-colored man, Black Guinea, John Ringman, and so on. But though they share certain kinds of behavior, these individuals are distinct from one another. Thus it is not quite accurate to say, as Hennig Cohen does, that "they are identical, a single actor playing a number of different roles."[9] To use the old device of the general semanticists, Confidence-Man_1 is not Confidence-Man_2 is not Confidence-Man_3.

I agree, then, with H. Bruce Franklin's interpretation of Melville's device. As Franklin says, "If we are presented with a character described as a crippled Negro beggar on a Mississippi riverboat, we expect that character to remain the same except as he is changed by circumstances we are told about or may infer. He may get off the boat, stop begging, become healed, or, even more miraculously, lose his identity as a Negro; but he changes only as we accept the author's manipulations. If, in the next chapter, there appears a character who does not *appear* to be the same character, he *is* not the same character unless and until we are convinced that he is."[10]

Language, of course, *is* linked to the world, but only by convention. Usage—human behavior—provides the indirect connection between words and things. If we

[9]Hennig Cohen, in his edition of Herman Melville, *The Confidence-Man* (New York, 1964), p. xi.

[10]H. Bruce Franklin, in his edition of *The Confidence-Man* (New York, 1967), p. xx.

want to know whether or not aspirin is a dangerous drug, we find out not by staring at an aspirin tablet or by looking up the word in a dictionary but by asking how people behave when they take it. In short, language "functions because someone, including ourselves, is attempting to control our behavior."[11] And this is what the "wordy" Confidence-Man does, again and again, in Melville's book. He doesn't really bilk people out of much money, but he does press them to put their money where their mouth is; money, like language, is a transfer agent, a translator and amplifier whose significance is conventional but nonetheless real. As anyone knows who has tried to use cash when a credit card is called for, a card of identity may be more important than money. Marshall McLuhan has appropriately called cash "the poor man's credit card."

From one point of view, then, *The Confidence-Man* appears to be the bleak, nihilistic book that most of its interpreters have described. When Mark Winsome says to the cosmopolitan in chapter 36, "What are you? What am I? Nobody knows who anybody is," he sums up Melville's forlorn conclusions concerning "everything that lies beyond human ken." The world itself is unstable, our sign systems for describing it neither match it nor are they themselves stable, and both the world and the sign systems are subject to various unstable interpretations. As the interpolated narratives in the book remind us, what we call "reality" is like fiction in being man-made. The reality of ordinary life is an intricate social

[11]Peckham, *The Triumph of Romanticism,* p. 295.

construction maintained by routines, institutionalization, habitual role-playing, and legitimation.[12] But its apparent solidity is abruptly challenged when we realize that, like Melville's pilgrims, we are all transients headed for the Terminal and that, like the old man at the end of the book, we are going to be "kindly" led away.

To be a little less apocalyptic about it, the appearance of a stranger not only introduces the question of whether he can be trusted but also implies the larger question: Can anyone or any institution be trusted? As the cosmopolitan says to the barber (whose sign reads "No Trust"), "To say that strangers are not to be trusted, does not that imply something like saying that mankind is not to be trusted; for the mass of mankind, are they not necessarily strangers to each individual man?" The acid test of confidence or faith, or course, is the problem of evil. If God is omnipotent and all-good, why then does he permit the existence of evil in the world? If nature is benevolent, why do we have tornadoes, eathquakes, and floods? And if man is perfectible or unstained at birth, why then is he so mean, greedy, and hypocritical? In this book man is damned if he believes and damned if he doesn't—and not even exegesis saves.

That outrageous pun leads us to another aspect of the book that is dialectically opposed to the one we have just outlined. To recognize that words are not chained to the world, that fiction is not limited to representing reality,

[12]Berger and Luckmann, *The Social Construction of Reality,* pp. 72–79.

and that identity is not ordained by nature or God is in one sense to be liberated: free to play with words, stories, and roles. Life becomes "a picnic *en costume*" in which "one must take a part, assume a character, stand ready in a sensible way to play the fool." Though Melville was deeply depressed in 1856 when he told Hawthorne that he had "pretty much made up his mind to be annihilated," he must have had fun writing this book.[13] With its puns and cross-talk, its elaborate philosophizing, the dumping of plot and rounded characters, the relentless telling of stories within stories, *The Confidence-Man* is a grimly exuberant April Fool's joke, anticipating the verbal and fictive ingenuities of John Barth and Vladimir Nabokov. But what a shrinkage accompanies this apparent freedom! It is as if a man-sized Sisyphus, recognizing the absurdity of pushing his own reifications up the hill, has recognized that he can at least laugh off his role and, free (temporarily) from the institutionalized reality of ordinary life, become a diminutive Proteus.

Part of man's minuteness stems from his inability to understand causation and his consequent inability to control his own future. Confronted with events that he does not understand, he can attribute them to chance, to Providence, to the devil, or not think about them at all. Given his aversion to chaos, he is likely to accept one of

[13]As Leon Howard indicates in his biography, Melville "had recovered, for a while, his mental equilibrium; and he was inclined to celebrate it with exuberance." See Leon Howard, *Herman Melville: A Biography* (Berkeley, 1951), pp. 230–37.

the last three options. And given the predominant misery in the world, the last two make the most sense. This, of course, is one of the points labored by Twain in *The Mysterious Stranger.* As the boy narrator, Theodor Fischer, says at the outset: "Mainly we were trained to be good Christians; to revere the Virgin, the Church, and the saints above everything. Beyond these matters we were not required to know much; and, in fact, not allowed to. Knowledge was not good for the common people, and could make them discontented with the lot which God had appointed for them, and God would not endure discontentment with his plans." Twain offers the reader a pan-determinism in which the ways of God are equated with the ways of Satan. The plot hinges around the discovery of eleven hundred and seven ducats by good Father Peter. The reader and the boys know that the money has been planted by young Satan. Father Peter and the rest of the community do not. "And there was no mystery; Father Peter told the whole circumstance just as it happened, and said that he could not account for it, only it was the plain hand of Providence, so far as he could see. One or two shook their heads and said privately it looked more like the hand of Satan; and really that seemed a surprisingly good guess for ignorant people like that."

Most readers now find Twain's book rather sophomoric, but his central motif is, after all, historically plausible. If we ask why the great witch hunts occurrred as late as the sixteenth century when the methods of scientific discovery were already well advanced (an estimated thirty-two hundred people were executed in southwest Germany between 1561 and 1670), one answer, as George Steiner has suggested, is that the witchcraft, as well as the torture and murder of human beings thought to be witches, is inseparable from Christianity itself. . . . The notion of the Devil and of a perpetual menace of infernal seduction are inherent in the Christian world picture."[14] Perhaps the reason *The Mysterious Stranger* seems tame today is that Twain avoids the sexual aspects of witchcraft and the cannibalistic connotations enacted in the sacrament of Holy Communion. More probably, after Auschwitz, Vietnam, Jonestown, or whatever latest outbreak of racial or religious hatred, we have become immunized against outrage in the face of hideousness.

Philip Traum's long tirade at the end of Twain's story, in which he utters the word "strange" three times and convinces Theodor Fischer that the world as perceived by conventional Christians can be only a dream, a fiction, is not far removed from the observation of the sociologists Berger and Luckmann: "The thought keeps suggesting itself (the 'insane' thought par excellence) that, perhaps, the bright reality of everyday life is but an illusion, to be swallowed up at any moment by the howling nightmares of the other, the night-side reality."[15] The function of Twain's story—to contain terror by ordering it in the socializing language of everyday life—has been taken over by newspaper headlines and television news. But the efforts of rational historians and sci-

[14]George Steiner, *New Yorker* 51 (September 8, 1975): 123–24.
[15]Berger and Luckmann, *The Social Construction of Reality,* p. 98.

entific analysis to fathom mass hysteria or fantasies of the devil remain inadequate. The long nightmare goes on, and stories of the strangers within and without will continue to be written.

They also serve who only stand and wait.
Milton, "On His Blindness"

Who's the bull goose loony here?
Ken Kesey, *One Flew over the Cuckoo's Nest*

4

Testing the Power

As we have seen in a story like "The Stout Gentleman," the response to strange intrusion may be simply mild curiosity as long as the insider or insiders are not threatened. But when the problem of knowing is coupled with a threat of destruction or displacement, as it usually is, the tension mounts. The basic question is one of power, who has it, and how it is to be controlled. In our stories this question expresses itself more specifically in some tentative combination of interrelated and dynamic polarities, the fundamental one being the clash between the stationary and the migratory. I say "stationary" rather than the more usual "sedentary" because it captures the militant stance of the slogan mentioned earlier: "Let's stay and keep [kick] the bastards out!"

Hawthorne's "The Gray Champion" provides an early example of this motif. There are the townspeople, temporarily cowed but earnestly desiring a community that will permit the maximum fruition of their individual lives; an outlaw-tyrant within, whose political and military power threatens the extinction of these individual freedoms for the sake of order; and a virile champion who miraculously intervenes to save the community. Though Hawthorne's treatment of the theme is relatively simple, he characteristically suggests some of the ambiguities latent in this situation. The townspeople are held together by a religious faith in their righteous cause; they retain some of the original Puritan spirit that united them when "threatened by some peril from the wilderness." But they include some "veterans of King Philip's war, who had burned villages and slaughtered young and old, with pious fierceness, while the godly souls throughout the land were helping them with prayer."

The oppressive British governor, Sir Edmund Andros, and his villainous associates are presented with no redeeming features. But the advance of their mercenary troops is described in a way that establishes the link between "progress" and the development of military technology. "Their steady march was like the progress of a machine, that would roll irresistibly over everything in its way." In this respect they do not differ from the colonists who, as Hawthorne reminds us elsewhere, laid their main streets "over the red man's grave." Both the colonists and their oppressors rely on the same kind of power; the difference, of course, is that Andros and his lackeys are abnormal growths upon the body politic. Hawthorne's tableau of these excrescences represents "the deformity of any government that does not grow out of the nature of things and the character of the people."

The Gray Champion has many of the characteristics

later to become standard in the western hero.[1] Like an ancient Gary Cooper he walks with gray but unbroken dignity toward the inevitable confrontation. His phallic weapon is a staff, not a six-gun, but he takes his position at the typical twenty-yard distance as he cries, "Stand!" Not quite as laconic as his modern avatars, the Gray Champion nevertheless chooses his words with precision and archaic dignity: "Back thou that wast a Governor, back! With this night thy power is ended—tomorrow, the prison!—back, lest I foretell the scaffold!" The stance and voice of the mysterious old man stir the souls of the people; they are ready to confront the soldiers and "convert the very stones of the street into deadly weapons." There is the muted suggestion—even though it must be rejected because it comes only from Andros and his men—that imprudence is madness, that the old man's behavior is insane. Finally, there is something elegiac about his disappearance. Like Shane, he fades slowly from the scene; "the men of that generation watched for his reappearance, in sunshine and in twilight, but never saw him more."

"I'll Take my Stand" is a refrain that echoes through American writing from Melville's "The Lightning-Rod Man", through the pronouncement of the southern agrarians in 1930, to Flannery O'Connor's "The Displaced Person." In the latter, as in "Noon Wine," the central relationship is between a settled employer and a migrant worker. The boss is able to stay put; the worker can

[1]See John G. Cawelti. *The Six-Gun Mystique* (Bowling Green, Ky., 1971).

always be told to move on. Or can he? This is the question raised in "Bartleby the Scrivener."

One of the story's central ironies is that the lawyer-narrator, himself an eminently safe man snugly ensconced in his Wall Street office, is displaced by a stranger whose quiet immobility becomes virtually pathological. Bartleby's preference neither to work in nor to leave the office is, of course, comprehensible when we consider the dehumanizing routine of the work. Confronted by the demand that they be copying machines all day long, the other employees respond by eating ginger-cakes all the time, by fiddling with their desks, by drinking at noon, by performing capably only half the time. Nippers is worthless in the morning, Turkey erratic and irascible in the afternoon. The strain emerges most notably in the ironic puns and doubletalk that link the passive activity of copying with the physical stasis of their job. Here, for example, is the boss's response to one of Turkey's aberrations: "Rashest of all the fiery afternoon blunders and flurried rashnesses of Turkey, was his once moistening a ginger-cake between his lips, and clapping it on to a mortgage, for a seal. I came within an ace of dismissing him then. But he mollified me by making an oriental bow, and saying—'With submission, sir, it was generous of me to find you in stationery on my own account.'"

This piece of gobbledygook is followed later in the story by a pathetic but hilarious dialogue between Bartleby and the lawyer, now at his wit's end:

> "'Well, then, would you like to travel through the country collecting bills for the merchants? That would improve your health.'"

"'No, I would prefer to be doing something else.'"

"'Now, then, would going as a companion to Europe, to entertain some young gentleman with your conversation—how would that suit you?'"

"'Not at all. It does not strike me that there is anything definite about that. I like to be stationary. But I am not particular.'"

"'Stationary you shall be, then,' I cried, now losing all patience. . . ."

A good photocopy-machine salesman could have solved the lawyer's problems, though his machine would have added new ones. I mention this technological anachronism because it leads us to a third aspect of the dialectic between the stationary and the migratory. To be settled—in an office, a town, or a home—is to be a potential customer or consumer, receptive and vulnerable to the pitch of a traveling salesman. For the ills of humanity he offers health, security, and salvation: a lightning rod, a Pain Dissuader, an Omni-Balsamic Reinvigorator, a Life Preserver, a way to salvation through the Bible. At the very least he promises relief from the boredom of routine drudgery. From Melville's "The Lightning-Rod Man" and *The Confidence-Man* to Steinbeck's "The Chrysanthemums" and Flannery O'Connor's "Good Country People," American short fiction has been rich in encounters between sly salesmen and rural, often resistant, victims.[2] Prudence counsels distrust of strangers; but, as Melville reminds us, to distrust a stranger is to reject part of humanity and ultimately part of ourselves.

[2]See Herschel Parker, "Melville's Salesman Story," *Studies in Short Fiction* 1 (Fall 1963): 154–56.

The most spectacular example of this essentially comic genre or subgenre is Faulkner's "Spotted Horses." The opening scene follows the conventions we have outlined earlier. Into the sleepy but restless hamlet of Frenchman's Bend ride two strangers in a covered wagon, leading "a considerable string of obviously alive objects which in the levelling sun resembled vari-sized and -colored tatters torn at random from large billboards." One of the men turns out to be no stranger; it is Flem Snopes, Faulkner's grotesque version of the Tyrant Within. The other is a true outsider, a Texan later identified as Buck Hipps, who wears "a densely black moustache, a wide pale hat," and a pearl-handled pistol. They are greeted with wary, humorous comment by the stationary natives lounging around the front of the store.

The new arrivals are the three sources of power in the story. The ultimate intruders are the horses (A Mysterious Horse story), and Faulkner does for them what Melville did for whales—he conveys an awesome sense of their unbridled energy. They rip, they soar, they surge, flow, crash though houses, and finally prove to be, like Moby Dick, "uncatchable." They are a "kaleidoscopic maelstrom of long teeth and wild eyes and slashing feet"; Faulkner compares them to partridges flushing, hysterical fish, banjo-faced jackrabbits, phantoms, Christmas pinwheels, "mad tossing shapes like a downrush of flames," a "gaudy vomit of long wild faces and splotched chests."

Mediating temporarily between the horses and the townsmen is the Texan. Calmly munching gingersnaps during his stay at Frenchman's Bend, he is notable first for his physical strength and skill in controlling the horses. Here is how he "gentles" one of them:

> For an instant it and the man appeared to be inextricable in one violence. Then they became motionless. The stranger's high heels dug into the earth, one hand gripping the animal's nostrils, holding the horse's head wrenched half around while it breathed in hoarse, smothered groans. "See?" the stranger said in a panting voice, the veins standing white and rigid in his neck and along his jaw. "See? All you got to do is handle them a little and work hell out of them for a couple of days."

Although some doubt is cast upon this statement when one of the other horses slashes at Hipps and splits his vest from collar to hem, the Texan remains undaunted and drives the horses into the lot behind Mrs. Littlejohn's house where they will be auctioned off.

Having temporarily controlled the horses, Hipps now proceeds to manipulate the men. He is a master auctioneer, trading on their contagious gullibility and the appeal of potent horseflesh:

> "Now boys," the Texan said. "Who says that pony aint worth fifteen dollars? You couldn't buy that much dynamite for just fifteen dollars. There aint one of them cant do a mile in three minutes; turn them into pasture and they will board themselves; work them like hell all day and every time you think about it, lay them over the head with a single-tree and after a couple of days every jack rabbit one of them will be so tame you will have to put them out of the house at night like a cat."

But when the most obsessed of the bidders, Henry Armstid, pays the family's last five dollars and then beats his wife for failing to help him capture his horse, the Texan intervenes on her behalf and gives her back the money. Although this noble gesture fails when Armstid insists on buying the horse and gives the money to Flem Snopes, Hipps's kindness to Mrs. Armstid establishes his dual role. He is Snopes's agent, helping him bilk the townsmen, but he is chivalrous. And he accepts his role with self-irony. Sitting in the fancy buggy with the fringed parasol top that Flem has procured for him, he rides off—not back home where he "wouldn't get past the first Texas saloon without starting the vigilance Committee," but to "look-see them Northern towns. Washington and New York and Baltimore.'"

Lurking behind the physical power of the horses and the skills of the Texan is the man who really controls the whole situation, the satanic Flem Snopes. When he refuses to give Mrs. Armstid back her five dollars and gives her instead a bag of candy for her children—"a little sweetening for the chaps"—we sense that the horses were his, the money is his, and the power is his. As Lump Snopes, addressing the men in the store, says of Flem: "'You might as well to quit. . . . You can't beat him.'" They can't beat him, partly because they are gullible and partly because they are bored. Will Varner sums up their mood:

> You take a man that aint got no other relaxation all year long except dodging mule-dung up and down a field furrow. And a night like this one, when a man aint old enough yet to lay still and sleep, and yet he aint young enough anymore to be tomcatting in and out of other folks' back windows, something like this is good for him. It'll make him sleep tomorrow night anyhow, provided he get back home by then.

If the routine is boring for the men, it is reality for the women. Throughout the long day the madness at the lot has been juxtaposed with the calm, slightly cold practicality of Mrs. Littlejohn, whose frequent appearances in her backyard to get wood or ring the bell for meals indicate that, for her, at least, life goes on as usual.

The same weird blending of chaos and calm, of sane madness and irrational sanity marks the concluding trial scene in which the case against Flem is dismissed and his victory is complete. As the justice drily intones the technicalities of the law, Mrs. Tull, at first calm and quiet—"too calm and quiet"—begins shouting at her husband, the bailiff roars " 'Order! Order!' " and the old justice finally cries: " 'This court's adjourned! Adjourned!' "

Instead of peddling objects, organic or mechanical, the stranger may move more directly to the heart of civilized corruption by offering easy money. And when a whole community is involved, the test of power usually comes in a trial or a town meeting. Twain's *The Mysterious Stranger* and "The Man That Corrupted Hadleyburg" are the most familiar examples.

The basic plot device in both stories involves the link between language and money, a connection that Twain knew all too well, not from thoughtful study but from painful personal experience. Money talks; but for Twain, more than for most other men, talk was money: the way out of debt was not just the published word but the oral performance. So in *The Mysterious Stranger* young Satan melts into Wilhelm Meidling in the trial scene, makes him a crisp, competent lawyer, and changes the dates on the coins to prove that they could not have possibly belonged to the astrologer. "The money could speak, after all." In "The Man That Corrupted Hadleyburg," as the pronoun in the title suggests, the stranger is a mere mechanical device, a way of releasing the corruption in the "incorruptible" town. Again the instrument is money, coupled with a "test remark." Twain apparently enjoyed what the modern reader is likely to find tedious: the complex manipulation of funds, the pun between "guilt" and "gilt," and the parody of religious and patriotic ritual in the town meeting. In both stories we are left with the sardonic conclusion that in a power-ridden, corrupt world the few who are "saved"—Father Peter and the Richardses—go crazy.

A traveler, even if he is a salesman, is also a guest. In the hands of a greedy host it is the migrant who is bilked. The question of who pays is a token pointing to the larger issue of whether power rests with those who serve and stand and wait or with those who move restlessly on. And this encounter becomes intensified in those historical moments when advancing civilization clashes with declining primitivism. John Cawelti has defined this "epic moment" as an essential ingredient of the western story and has further suggested that the conflict is always conditioned by our knowledge that it is always in some sense a fiction. The violence, after all, is contained in movies, books, television—a proof of advancing civilization. "The frontier setting now provided a fictional justification for enjoying violent conflicts and the expression of lawless force without feeling that they threatened the values or the fabric of society."[3]

In Crane's "The Blue Hotel" the power of fictional illusion becomes a self-fulfilling prophecy. The stranger, a Swede from New York, finds himself a displaced person in the alien environment of Fort Romper, Nebraska. Convinced by his reading of dime novels that he is in the wild West, he imagines himself as its potential victim. Later, aided by alcohol, he becomes a kind of assassin, thumping the "soul" out of one man and attacking another; the final result is that he becomes a real victim, a corpse alone in the saloon, its eyes fixed on the cash register. Thanks in part to his expectations, the stereotype of the violent West has become a reality.

I say "in part" because even at the outset the Swede's apparently absurd intuition is partly correct. His myth of the wild West conflicts with Scully's myth of Fort Romper as a civilized "met-tro-*pol*-is" complete with four churches, a big brick schoolhouse, and proposed electric streetcars. At its center is his own hotel, a warm temple of hospitality where the privileges of his guests are sacred. The facts are that his son Johnnie is cheating and quarreling with the old farmer over a card game, the gambler at the saloon is carrying a knife, and a savage storm is raging outside. The clash between these two orientations results in a progressive shift of power from Scully, the initial authority figure, to the Swede, and finally to the gambler.[4]

[3]Cawelti, *The Six-Gun Mystique,* p. 38.

[4]Robert Gleckner, "Stephen Crane and the Wonder of Man's Conceit," *Modern Fiction Studies* 5 (Autumn 1959): 271–81.

Like Scully, the main character in Frank Rooney's "Cyclists' Raid" is a host, a hotel owner. But the situation Joel Bleeker faces is more like that of the western where "the townspeople hover defensively in their settlement, threatened by the outlaws or Indians who are associated with the inhospitable and uncontrollable elements of the surrounding landscape. The townspeople are static and largely incapable of movement beyond their little settlement. The outlaws or savages can move freely across the landscape."[5] Though this is a modern version in which the Indians/outlaws are motorcyclists, the basic pattern remains the same. Again a small town is invaded by a horde of outsiders; again the invasion releases irrational forces within the town; again there is a yearning for law and order coupled with sense of its impotence when confronted with senseless, contagious violence.

The outsiders have three interrelated sources of power. The most obvious (more spectacular, naturally, in the movie *The Wild One* than in its written source) is their technological horsepower, the throbbing roar of the motorcycles. When Joel Bleeker, the receptor and point-of-view character, first hears the sound, he thinks it might be a four-engined plane, and he even has "the fantastic notion that the plane was going to strike the hotel." Initially this mechanical energy is all the more impressive because it is under tight control. "The long stern column" of red motorcycles is led by one man, Gar Simpson, and they maneuver their bikes with rigid precision at his command. Finally, with their uniforms and

[5]Cawelti, *The Six-Gun Mystique,* p. 40.

especially their green goggles, they have the power of anonymity. Reflecting their origin in the city of urban sprawl, the men of Troop B of the Angeleno Motorcycle Club are a standardized clan "seeking in each other a willful loss of identity."

The mechanized energy, military discipline, and anonymity of this "private army" are set over against the apparently close-knit community of the town. The people know each other's names, addresses, personal history, and foibles: Francis LaSalle is copartner of LaSalle and Fleet, Hardware. Bleeker's past includes service as a lieutenant colonel during the war and the loss of his wife in a violent riding accident. His young daughter, Cathy, has something of her mother's "brittle independence." Timmons is "about thirty, somewhat coarse and intolerant, and a little embarrassed at being in love with a girl as young as Cathy." Campbell, the deputy sheriff, is tall but has "the arms and shoulders of a child beneath a foggy, bloated face." The static townspeople are vulnerable because they welcome the outsiders' money and because they are curious, "lured by the presence of something unusual in the town."

When all the cyclists except one—"the boy" who takes off his goggles and does not seem to belong—get drunk and out of control, the inevitable confrontation occurs. After his friend LaSalle has been slugged, Bleeker asks the deputy, "Can you do anything?" But what can Campbell do? Throw them all in jail? They all look alike. A double catastrophe follows: Cathy's murder and symbolic rape by an anonymous cyclist riding out of control in the hotel and the subsequent brutal beating of the innocent cyclist who returns. Just before he himself starts the beating of the boy, Bleeker asks him angrily: "'You were one of them. You could have done something. Why in God's name didn't you do it?'"[6] Having asked the insider and the outsider why they did not act, Bleeker finally distills the meaning of the long day's tragedy by brooding over his own strange behavior in both striking and shielding the boy. As he considers his wavering between control and abandon, he realizes, like so many of the receptors in our stories, that the stranger without is not far removed from the stranger within.[7] Avenging Cathy's death was perfectly natural—"as natural as a man drinking a few beers and riding a motorcycle insanely through a town like this. Bleeker shuddered. It might have been all right for a man like Timmons who was and would always be incapable of

[6]Some version of the refrain, "You could have done something," recurs in those cloistral stories where no authoritative insider says, in effect, "I'll take my stand." They are the complement of the standard refrain addressed to the traveling hero: "You've got to stop running sometime."

[7]Since the outsider so often reflects an aspect of the insider's identity, a summary of those stories in which the strangers are really doubles probably would belong in this chapter. But this topic has been so thoroughly examined that further discussion seems unnecessary. See Otto Rank, *The Double: A Psychoanalytic Study,* trans. and ed. Harry Tucker, Jr. (Chapel Hill, N.C., 1971); Ralph Tymms, *Doubles in Literary Psychology* (Cambridge, Mass., 1949); Robert Rogers, *A Psychoanalytic Study of the Double in Literature* (Detroit, 1970); Albert J. Guérard, ed., *Stories of the Double* (New York, 1967); and John T. Irwin, *Doubling and Incest/Repetition and Revenge: A Speculative Reading of Faulkner* (Baltimore, 1975).

thinking what he—Joel Bleeker—was thinking. It was not—and would never be—all right for him."

The complexity of the relationship between host and guest is suggested by the etymology of *host.* The word derives from Old French *hoste*; from Latin *hospes*, meaning "stranger, guest, host"; and from *hostis,* meaning "stranger," plus *potis,* meaning "able." And it is akin to Latin *hostia*, an expiatory victim or sacrifice. As these origins indicate, host and guest may change places, often under threat of force. The host becomes a hostage, a victim, as the migrant takes command. This pattern of action, all too common in real life during the past decade, is long familiar to us in stories like "The Killers" and plays like Sherwood's *The Petrified Forest* (1935).

Though melodramatic and somewhat dated (or remembered chiefly as Humphrey Bogart's first major vehicle), the Sherwood play beautifully exemplifies Erik Erikson's reflections on the American identity. "In this country," says Erikson, "the migrant does not want to be told to move on, nor the sedentary man to stay where he is; for the life style (and the family history) of each contains the opposite element as a potential alternative which he wishes to consider his most private and individual decision."[8]

The play's action occurs at a lonely crossroad in Arizona in the lunchroom of the Black Mesa Filling Station and Bar-B-Q. The Maple family tend the place, all of them unhappy with their station in life. Jason, who

[8]Erikson, *Childhood and Society,* p. 286.

finds his only real status with the American Legion, wants to sell out and buy a barbecue service in Los Angeles; his daughter, Gabrielle, yearns to go to Europe where her French mother lives. As Gramp Maple, the ancient owner, says, "Ain't they nobody around here that's satisfied to stay put?" Jason retorts: "How about yourself? Were you ever satisfied to stay put, until you got so damned old you didn't have enough energy to move?" Even the helper, Boze Hertzlinger, dreams of leaving this Godforsaken place, remembering his glorious days as a broken-field runner for Nevada Tech. Gramp says: "The trouble with this country is, it's got settled. It's camped down in the bed of a dried-up river, and whenever anybody says 'let's get the hell out of here,' all the rest start to holler, 'If we move a step the Injuns'll get us.'"

If the inhabitants of the station are doomed to ossify at Black Mesa, their visitors seem condemned to purposeless travel. Two qualify as mysterious strangers: Alan Squier (originally played by Leslie Howard), a failed writer and romantic wanderer whose residence in Europe, "afterglow of elegance," and artistic temperament make him attractive to Gabrielle; and Duke Mantee, unshaven leader of a band of outlaws who have just killed six people in Oklahoma City. Squier and Mantee are about the same age, and they share at least one quality: both are "unmistakably condemned," aristocratic anachronisms in this middle-class society. The outlaws make hostages of the insiders, Squier puts purpose into his empty life by making over his life insurance to Gabrielle so that she can go to France, asks Mantee to kill him, and dies happy, buried in the Petrified Forest. After a wild shootout with deputies and legionnaires, Mantee and most of his men drive off into the night. But their ways out are limited; we know that they will be caught.

Around our original polarity of the stationary and the migratory have clustered the often reciprocal roles of employer and worker, customer and salesman, host and guest. With some trepidation we now add the traditional and emotion-laden distinction between feminine and masculine. In the past it was possible, even common, to see this division as the basic one in life and in fiction. So Walter S. Campbell could write that there are two fundamental narratives. One is the "foundation plot of all tales of adventure, of brave men and daring enterprise—in short the story of Man. For man is centrifugal, the wanderer and fighter, the lover of danger and distance: Achilles, Odysseus." The other is "the foundation plot of many of the best stories of endurance—in short, the story of Woman. . . . She is centripetal, she stays and bears it."[9] Examples are Griselda, Cinderella, Melville's projected story of Agatha. Or one thinks of Faulkner's Dilsey, who endured. Or Campbell's mention of centripetal and centrifugal force may remind us of Henry Adams's famous description of the Virgin and the Dynamo. Or we may heed those who have said that there are, fundamentally, only two stories: Cinderella and Jack and the Bean

[9]Walter S. Campbell, *Writing Magazine Fiction* (New York, 1940), pp. 60–61.

Stalk."[10] Or I could cite my own earlier comments in an interpretation of Hawthorne's fiction. There I wrote that man speculates, "penetrates into space and is a master of locomotion," whereas woman invests; "her natural role is to clothe and conserve in time."[11] (I still think this is an accurate description of Hawthorne's views, but I wish now that I had achieved a little more distance between his and my own.) Or, finally, there is Erik Erikson's report of a famous experiment in which little boys use their toys and blocks to construct outdoor scenes of action and collision, whereas little girls prefer static interiors that are "peaceful or intruded upon." From this experiment Erikson concluded that, although each sex can learn to imitate the modes of the other, the "spatial phenomena observed here . . . express two principles of arranging space which correspond to the male and female principles in body construction" and that these are "relevant throughout life to the elaboration of sex-roles in cultural space-times."[12]

The most lucid and sensible argument against accepting the primacy of sexual differences, whether one is classifying fiction or defining "ego-identity," is found in Elizabeth Janeway's *Man's World, Woman's Place.* As she says, her book is "not a polemic, but an inquiry." What the inquiry reveals, though, is that around the undeni-

[10]R. V. Cassill, *Writing Fiction* (New York, 1962), p. 18. Cassill mentions this notion without necessarily supporting it.

[11]Roy R. Male, *Hawthorne's Tragic Vision* (Austin, Texas, 1957), p. 7.

[12]Eric Erikson, *Childhood and Society,* 2d ed. (New York, 1963), pp. 106, 270–71, 273.

able difference in male and female body plans has been built an imposing social mythology. Here is her trenchant introductory premise:

> Let us grant what I don't believe, that there are innate or "genetically conditioned" differences in the psychological makeup of the sexes. The result is much the same, for these differences cannot be instinctive, they cannot lie just where we believe them to be today, or why must they also be taught—and taught with more sternness than goes into most present-day education? Why do variations from them make us so uneasy—more uneasy than the sight of physical crippling? If we are sure that sexual roles are innate and inherited, why do we treat homosexuals as if they had willfully chosen to be deviates? Above all, why do our standards of behavior for sex roles change from generation to generation and region to region? They exist in every society, but the difference between them is always a little different. Woman's place is always on the map, but it shifts about. Since the underlying physical arrangements don't shift, we have to assume that the changes in what we think about them are just that—changes in what we think. We have to posit a social mythology.[13]

Janeway's analysis of that mythology confirms what we have already observed in our study of cloistral fiction—that those who stay in their place are not necessarily women and those who travel out in the world seeking a career. like Dreiser's Carrie Meeber, are not necessarily men. But, as Janeway shows, it is a mistake to dismiss as absurd various categorical statements about masculinity and femininity simply because they are cul-

[13]Elizabeth Janeway, *Man's World, Woman's Place: A Study in Social Mythology* (New York, 1971), p. 10.

turally determined with little or no basis in biological or psychological evidence. The fact that those statements originate in fear and fantasy, far from making them irrelevant, may indeed make them more powerful.

Whether the idea is rational or not, there *is* something about a passive posture that is associated in American fiction, as in its culture, with femininity. The hit men in "The Killers," togged out in their tight-fitting overcoats and sawed-off shotguns, emphasize this stereotyping in their contemptuous comments. Max says to George: "'He can cook and everything. You'd make some girl a nice wife, bright boy.'" And Al says of his hostages: "'I've got them tied up like a couple of girl friends in the convent.'" Even a man of status, the lawyer in "Bartleby," feels "unmanned" somehow when he is confronted by the mystery of intrusion and displacement.

Even in those cloistral stories in which the primary test of power is sexual, the attraction of the man seems more often than not to be linked with his mobility. In Steinbeck's "The Chrysanthemums," for example, Eliza Allen, comfortably married but restless in her passive relationship with her husband, pours her excess energy into cultivating chrysanthemums. When the stranger, an unprepossessing itinerant tinker, appears at the farm, she is attracted to him because his dark, brooding eyes suggest the unpredictability of a roving existence. He says: "'I ain't in no hurry ma'am. I go from Seattle to San Diego and back every year. Takes all my time. I aim to follow nice weather.'" And he has a gift with words: he remembers that chrysanthemum blooms look "'like a quick puff of colored smoke.'" Though she is temporarily repelled by his sales pitch, he appeals to her again when he asks if he can take some chrysanthemum sprouts to a customer down the road. She pulls off her battered hat, shakes out her dark pretty hair, and prepares the plants in a state of sexual excitement.

For one moment in the scene that follows the two share a mood of erotic mysticism. The tinker seems to understand the complexity of Eliza's sensual response:

> "Maybe I know," he said. "Sometimes in the night in the wagon there—" Eliza's voice grew husky. She broke in on him. "I've never lived as you do. but I know what you mean. When the night is dark—why, the stars are sharp-pointed, and there's quiet. Why, you rise up and up! Every pointed star gets driven into your body. It's like that. Hot and sharp and lovely."

Both the sexual undertones of this outburst and Eliza's subsequent physical advance toward the tinker are probably unconsciously motivated.[14] And when the stranger, somewhat embarrassed by her strange behavior, breaks the mood with the realistic comment that it's not so nice in the wagon when there's nothing to eat, Eliza retreats into her role of normal housewife. After giving him some battered pots to fix and paying him for the repairs, she says good-by. But the romantic aura of the itinerant remains as she whispers to herself: " 'That's a bright direction. There's a glowing there.' "

By the end of the story the glow of romance is gone.

[14]Elizabeth E. McMahan, " 'The Chrysanthemums' " A Study of a Woman's Sexuality," *Modern Fiction Studies* (Winter 1968): 453–58.

Having ritualistically cleansed herself after the encounter with the tinker, Eliza puts on her prettiest dress and prepares for the promised trip to town with her husband. On the road she sees a dark speck far ahead, and she knows what it will be. "The tinker has discarded her chrysanthemums, symbol of the femininity which she hopes will inspire the excitement she longs for. But he has kept the pot—an insult on any level of interpretation, to discard her treasure and keep its utilitarian container."[15] Angry at first, she momentarily considers going to the prizefight and watching men hurt each other. Then she subsides in her place, "crying weakly—like an old woman." Steinbeck's story shows us how it feels when the myth of female power fluctuates with the myth of female weakness.

Callous though he is, Steinbeck's tinker is less malicious than most of the other vagrant demon-lovers in our canon. There is one-armed Tom T. Shiftlet in Flannery O'Connor's "The Life You Save May Be Your Own," who arrives at Mrs. Crater's desolate farm, greets the old woman and her retarded daughter, Lucynell, spots a rusty old car and asks, "'You ladies drive?'" During the grotesque bargaining that ensues, Mrs. Crater offers him "'a permanent house and a deep well and the most innocent girl in the world,'" adding that "'there ain't any place in the world for a poor disabled friendless drifting man.'" Shiftlet's cool response to this offer of permanency is couched in metaphysical terms. "'Lady,'" he says, "'a man is divided into two parts,

[15]Ibid., p. 458.

body and spirit. . . . The body, lady, is like a house, it don't go anywhere; but the spirit, lady, is like a automobile: always on the move.'" A resounding simile, but, like the motorists' slogan which supplies the title of the story, it contains the tension between Christian and contemporary values that is basic in O'Connor's fiction. This crooked Christ's values, after all, are just as materialistic as Mrs. Crater's. After considerable hilarious mutual deception they arrive at a bargain. He will marry the idiot daughter in exchange for the car, a paint job, and $17.50. Mobilized, he races off toward Mobile, abandoning Lucynell—the "angel of Gawd"—at a lunchroom called The Hot Spot.

On the road Shiftlet is haunted by what he has done, but he is functioning now according to his own flawed idea of right living, a sentimental longing for mother and an absurd sense that he, who has abandoned the hopeless, is a responsible man because he stops for a hitchiker. The boy is Shiftlet's intruder, violently rejecting his claptrap illusions. That and his own sense of what he has done push him to realization: you may not save your own life. "Mr. Shiftlet felt that the rottenness of the world was about to engulf him. He raised his arm and let it fall again to his breast. 'Oh Lord!' he prayed. 'Break forth and wash the slime from this earth!'"[16]

No reader can miss the religious dimension in O'Connor's fiction, though what it finally means will probably be debated to the point of exhaustion. All I am em-

[16]I am indebted in this paragraph to an unpublished paper by Linda Miller.

phasizing here is that even in a story like "Good Country People," which ostensibly deals with a sexual encounter (a variant of the old dirty jokes about the traveling salesman and the farmer's daughter), the real clash is between feminine characters whose lives are stable and claustrophobic and a masculine vagrant whose occupation as Bible salesman masks total impiety. He calls himself Manley Pointer, a name as appropriate as it is false, and his origin is " 'not even from a place, just from near a place.' " He intrudes into Mrs. Hopewell's house, gradually establishing himself as a "good country person." She resists his pitch at first, but the sentimental clichés that serve as her world view prompt her to invite him to dinner when she learns that he has a heart condition like her daughter's. They *do* both have heart conditions: Joy-Hulga, with her Ph.D. and her wooden leg, is an example of the dogged, ugly, deformed rationalists for whom O'Connor seems to reserve a special, scathing wrath. Hulga determines to seduce this simple country boy and in the process introduce his unsophisticated mind to her belief in nothingness. He invites her for a walk in the woods, " 'o'er the hills and far away,' " and then they retire to the second story of a storage barn.

Thus begins the notorious and unforgettable seduction scene in which Pointer exposes the limits of her nihilism to Hulga by exceeding it. The wooden leg is necessary to Hulga, as she discovers when she is seduced into removing it. "It was like losing her own life and finding it again, miraculously, in his." This feeling, however, is just a sneaky perversion of the real surrender to grace. Hulga is depending on Pointer's innocent interest in her precious leg; her courage to "see *through* to nothing" fails in the face of whiskey, dirty cards, and contraceptives. To get back the leg she appeals to those pieties of her mother which she has scornfully denied: "'Aren't you . . . just good country people? . . . You're a Christian!'" But the clichés are no more useful than her rational nihilism in the face of real demonic nothingness. Pointer leaves her immobilized, physically and philosophically: "'And I'll tell you another thing, Hulga . . . you ain't so smart. I been believing in nothing ever since I was born' and then the toast-colored hat disappeared down the hole and the girl was left, sitting on the straw in the dusty sunlight."

Surveying two negative roles of loving—the bitch and the Don Juan—Elizabeth Janeway writes that "the old double-standard pattern of sex allows the Don to couple in man's world with impunity, for if a woman strays out there it's her own fault. She should have stayed in her own place, with her male kin to protect her."[17] This description fits the testing pattern in Joyce Carol Oates's story "Where Are You Going, Where Have You Been?" Connie, the fifteen-year-old protagonist, stays home on a Sunday morning while her parents and older sister go to a family barbecue. The strange traitor-lover who drives up to the house has his name printed on the side of his gold-painted open jalopy. It is "'Arnold Friend and that's my real name and I'm going to be your friend, honey.'" He is accompanied by another man (both are older than they first appear), whose name is

[17]Janeway, *Man's World, Woman's Place,* p. 202.

Ellie Oscar and is "'kinda strange.'" His transistor radio and Connie's inside the house are both tuned to the same program.

What follows, rendered through Connie's acute but disoriented senses, is Arnold Friend's prolonged effort to lure her out of the house and into the car. He succeeds for several reasons. He is able to convince her that her refuge is fragile: "'The place you are now—inside your daddy's house—is nothing but a cardboard box I can knock down anytime.'" He threatens to harm her family if she doesn't leave before they return. And his incantatory voice, heard against the background of the driving rock music, appeals to her confused desire to be sexually attractive and to explore new experience. Half-hypnotized, she watches herself push open the door, heading for "so much land that Connie had never seen before and did not recognize except to know that she was going to it." What Connie half-consciously knows and what the reader certainly knows is that the land stretching before her will no longer be virgin; her prospect is rape.

Rape, castration—these real or feared violations of our private parts—are they the ultimate invasions of privacy? To them we would have to add not only the fear of madness and death so prominent in Poe's stories, and recurrent in cloistral fiction, but also incursions into the head: lobotomy, electric-shock treatment, electrical stimulation of the brain. Thus we are led to another polarity: the test of power between agent and patient.

The classic contemporary example, of course, is *One*

Flew over the Cuckoo's Nest. Kesey's novel contains virtually all the conventions of cloistral fiction: the enclosed setting, an insane asylum with its rigid routine; the receptor, Chief Bromden, Kesey's version of the Oldest Inhabitant (he has been in the ward longer than any of the other patients); the Tyrant Within, Big Nurse Ratched, whose name suggests, among other things, that she runs the machinery; the members of the crowd, tagged by the peculiarities of their illnesses; the mysterious intruder, Randle Patrick McMurphy, con man and Christ figure; the breakout in the form of a fishing trip; the contagiousness first of distrust and weakness and later of power; and the duel.

The first duel is between McMurphy and Harding, prompted by Mack's question: "'Who's the bull goose loony here?'" It's a mock shootout, quickly settled. McMurphy says, "'Tell this Harding that he either meets me man to man or he's a yaller skunk and better be out of town by sunset.'" And Harding replies, "'Bibbit, you tell this young upstart McMurphy that I'll meet him in the main hall at high noon and we'll settle this affair once and for all, libidos a-blazin'.'" McMurphy wins, but, as the chief says, "I'm not sure just what."

As the bull-goose loony, McMurphy is cast in the role of victim-savior. For the real power struggle is between his rugged individualism, his "man-smell of dust and dirt from the open fields, and sweat, and work," and the sterilizing force of Big Nurse, who runs the ward as agent for the Combine, Kesey's term for the Establishment that controls society. Against the formidable weapons of the Combine, McMurphy sets an example that gradually transforms the patients from their rabbit-like timidity into men.

Since most of the men were voluntary patients anyway, they leave the ward when Big Nurse loses her control over them. The process of releasing the power of spontaneous laughter, the power of madness, finally the power of manhood has by no means been easy or without human cost. Cheswick has drowned himself, Billy Bibbit has committed suicide, and McMurphy ultimately is lobotomized. But his power has been transferred to the Big Chief, who mercifully ends McMurphy's vegetable existence, rips loose the heavy control panel, throws it through the window, and heads for his home country.

No reader can miss the meaning of the novel. What is less easy to grasp is how Kesey was able to gain the approval of young radical readers in 1962 with a book whose deliberately stereotyped values were in many ways alien to theirs. The ever-present black aides, for instance, are part of the mechanized system, portrayed as minor villains throughout. And the attitude toward women in the novel is standard macho: Big Nurse is right out of Philip Wylie's caricature of Momism in *A Generation of Vipers,* and the way to manhood is aided by the two happy, good-hearted whores, Candy and Sandy. Why weren't more feminine readers outraged by this portrait of men as victims of a matriarchy—a matriarchy, furthermore, that had all the power of machinery on its side? This question leads us to our final polarity, one which is more highly specialized than any we have considered thus far and yet more experiential: the relation between reader and author. Chief Bromden says of

Nurse Ratched: "She couldn't rule with her old power any more, not by writing things on pieces of paper." Yet this, after all, is what a writer must do—and try to do with his "old power."

I'm going to be relying on you a good deal from now on, you see: for patience and understanding and all that; and so I thought I'd best start out by addressing you directly, though of course I realize it's an unusual way to begin a book. But it isn't the same as sticking my foot in your door, is it? I hope not; I've no desire to be unmannerly or overbearing—not like some of the young guys writing nowadays. You can always shut me out any time you want to, just by closing the book.

Hayden Carruth, *Appendix A*

"*Je est un autre,*" said Rimbaud. Another *I,* who has replaced my own, and who will continue to do so as long as I read. Reading is just that: a way of giving way not only to a host of alien words, images, ideas, but also to the very alien principle which utters them and shelters them.

Georges Poulet, "The Phenomenology of Reading"

5

The Curiously Receptive Reader and the Mysterious Author

To SOME EXTENT, the plot of the cloistral story and its characteristic themes of curiosity about the strange and uncertainty about power are ways of dramatizing the relation between reader and writer. Viewed from some distance, this interaction looks simple enough, but when analyzed more closely, it is puzzling. Does the text control the reader? If so, why isn't there more uniformity of response? Or does each reader in some way make his own meanings? If so, how can we account for the considerable amount of consensus that usually occurs? Some of the metaphors for this interaction indicate our apparent confusion on this point. On the one hand, we "digest," "devour," have a "taste" for certain books: on the other, we are "absorbed," "swept away," "enthralled," "gripped" by them. In academia perhaps the final irony is that critical essays on this problem have multiplied just as fewer students seem interested in reading.

Along with the distractions of other media, one reason for this lack of interest—in assigned reading at any rate—may well be the lingering influence of the New

Criticism in the classroom. Although their theoretical foundations are now generally recognized as being in ruins, the methods taught by Brooks, Warren, and their imitators remain in use partly because they are rather easily learned and portable. They are portable because the American formalists assume a more or less uniform response among readers of literature. I say "more or less," because the hypothetical readers' responses are usually subdivided into "more or less appropriate."[1] From the harried teacher's standpoint this spectrum of appropriateness can then be easily translated into letter grades, and the demands for objectivity are met. The frustrated student who insists that he should not be penalized because his interpretation disagrees with the teacher's is referred back to the text itself, that awesome verbal icon whose meaning cannot be paraphrased without heretical mutilation.[2]

Trained in the New Criticism myself, I am reluctant to see its corpse dragged slowly out of the classroom. As Whitman would say, it was "fittest for its days": it taught us to pay attention to the text, to make coherent statements about literature instead of merely learning history, discovering influences, or parroting some august critic's impressionistic account of his soul's adventures among masterpieces. But we now know (don't we?) that neither the "intentional fallacy" nor the "affective fal-

[1]See, for example, the labored commentary on "The Killers" in *Understanding Fiction,* ed. Cleanth Brooks and Robert Penn Warren, 2d ed. (New York, 1959), pp. 316–21.

[2]See David Bleich, "The Subjective Paradigm." *New Literary History* 7 (Winter 1976): 332–33; Norman Holland, *5 Readers Reading* (New Haven, Conn., 1975), 246–47, 281–83.

lacy" is really a fallacy (though those magisterial essays did usefully raise the crucial questions); that literary language does not differ inherently from ordinary language; and that readers' responses are neither uniformly nor simply controlled by the stimulus of a text.[3]

With the aid of those scholars who have been most articulate about these potentially explosive issues ("explosive" academically because if taken seriously their resolution could flatten the barriers now separating such departments as English, journalism, and psychology and shatter the grading system in many courses), let us examine the interaction between text and reader more closely and systematically. I say "text" and would like immediately to assume that it is a literary text. But what constitutes a literary text? How does it differ from some other kind of text? Because it is meant to please rather than to be used? Because its statements cannot be verified by any test except coherence? Because its language is more concrete, more polysemous, more reflexive, more deviant than ordinary language?

Let us turn first to our most graceful and persuasive theoretician, Northrop Frye. He argues that literary texts are distinguished from other verbal structures by "the absence of a controlling aim of descriptive accuracy." In descriptive or assertive writing the "final direc-

[3]The two essays on the "intentional fallacy" and the "affective fallacy" by William K. Wimsatt, Jr., and Monroe C. Beardsley are reprinted in *The Verbal Icon* (Lexington, Ky., 1954), pp. 3-18, 21-39. For refutation see Morse Peckham, *Man's Rage for Chaos: Biology, Behavior, and the Arts* (New York, 1965), pp. 126-27; Morse Peckham, *The Triumph of Romanticism,* (Columbia, S.C., 1970), pp. 421-44; and Holland, *5 Readers Reading,* pp. 1-12, 281-83.

tion is outward. . . . In all literary verbal structures the final direction of meaning is inward. . . . In literature questions of fact or truth are subordinated to the primary literary aim of producing a structure of words for its own sake, and the sign values of symbols are subordinated to their importance as a structure of interconnected motifs. Whenever we have an autonomous verbal structure of this kind, we have literature."[4] Or, as Wolfgang Iser more bluntly puts it, what is peculiar to all literary texts is that "they permit no referral to any identical real-life situation."[5] Fine. But what happens to Aristotle's *Poetics,* Boswell's *Life of Johnson,* Bradford's *History of Plymouth Plantation,* Milton's *Areopagitica,* Franklin's *Autobiography?* Jefferson's Declaration of Independence? Capote's *In Cold Blood?* Is the "final direction of meaning" in *The Education of Henry Adams* centrifugal or centripetal? Anthologies of English and American literature would have to be pruned radically if we were to adhere strictly to this definition.

Nevertheless, there is more to be said for it than for any of the attempts to distinguish literary language from ordinary discourse. We often read, for example, that literary language is identifiable by its concreteness. But what could be more concrete than the language of a phone book or a Sears catalog? And how concrete is the language at the beginning of Eliot's "Burnt Norton"?

[4]Northrop Frye, *The Anatomy of Criticism,* (Princeton, N.J., 1957), p. 74.

[5]Wolfgang Iser, "Indeterminacy and the Reader's Response in Prose Fiction," in *Aspects of Narrative,* ed. J. Millis Miller (New York, 1971), p. 8.

> Time present and time past
> Are both perhaps present in time future,
> And time future contained in time past.

Or we are told that literary language is more richly symbolic, more ambiguous, or more deviant than ordinary language. "Big Hans yelled, so I came out." Is that literary or nonliterary language? It is literary. How do I know? Because I remember that it is the first sentence of a short story by William Gass. How about this one: "There was a boy and a girl too this time." So far as I know, this is ordinary language—and vulnerable to an English teacher's marginal comment: "Agr." But "There was a man and a dog too this time" is, as everyone will agree, literary language because we remember it as the opening sentence of "The Bear."

In short we must grudgingly admit that literature like the other arts is a disjunctive category.[6] We recognize literary texts the way we recognize members of a club, not by any identical traits but by the social acceptance of their membership, attested to, if need be, by their membership cards. Whether or not a text is literary is a social convention, culturally determined (it is instructive in this connection to compare the *Cyclopedia of American Literature,* edited by the Duyckinck brothers in 1855, with any modern anthology).

Thus we are driven to Morse Peckham's "preliminary definition" of all art: "A work of art is what the perceiver observes in what has been culturally established as

[6]Jerome S. Bruner, *A Study of Thinking* (New York, 1956), p. 159. See also Peckham, *Man's Rage for Chaos,* pp. 47–49.

an art perceiver's space."[7] A fragment from *Soul on Ice* is literature if it is presented to a reader in an anthology of American literature; if John Ashbery calls a book *Three Poems,* they are poems even though both left- and right-hand margins are justified on the page.

Peckham goes further, however. Although we cannot find any defining attribute in a unique work of art, if we arrange in chronological sequence works or behavioral patterns that have been labeled artistic by various cultures, we notice that they exhibit a high degree of non-functional change. "Any object (or perceptual field) from any culture may, then, be properly categorized as having been the occasion for artistic perception if a chronologically arranged sequence of such objects shows both functional identity and non-functional stylistic dynamism."[8] Thus the primary role of the artist is that of providing violations of formal expectations; he offers the perceiver a protected way of exposing himself to future shock. "Art is the ingredient in human behavior which enables man to innovate, because it trains him to endure the cognitive tension which is the necessary preliminary to problem perception and genuine and meaningful innovation."[9]

Peckham's language is drawn from behavioristic psychology; in fact, he predicts that literary criticism will eventually find its proper place among the behavioral sciences. This is not a position that has won eager support from traditional literary humanists. But in shifting

[7]Peckham, *Man's Rage for Chaos*, p. 65.
[8]Ibid., p. 71.
[9]Peckham, *The Triumph of Romanticism,* p. 280.

attention away from the art work itself toward the roles of artist and art perceiver, Peckham laid the groundwork for the new attention to the process of reading. And for our purposes his model of the art-perceiving process is particularly useful since it closely resembles the typical plot of cloistral fiction.

The psychologists Peckham relies on suggest the following sequence in the ordinary perceptual situation: an organism's orientation or expectational set (roughly equivalent to our account of the priority of setting); cognitive tension as this orientation is confronted by phenomena it cannot handle or place (the intrusion of the strange); problem location; problem solving; feedback; corrected orientation and homeostasis. But, as Peckham points out, in ordinary life we seldom follow this whole sequence in attempting to reduce the tension between orientation and perceived phenomena. Instead we either ignore the new, inexplicable data or we find new ways of justifying our orientation. "The great human motto is, 'Millions for the orientation but not one cent for the reality.'"[10]

That is where the role of art is important for the behaviorist. It provides occasions for us to rehearse cognitive tension; works of art "train us to stand our ground when we encounter disorienting situations." Fiction, for example, begins by presenting a problem, something not readily comprehensible. "In normal behavior when a problem is encountered, the individual either suppresses awareness of it or devotes his energy to solving it. But fiction makes both impossible. On the

[10]Ibid., p. 264.

contrary, it postpones the solution of the problem and prevents its suppression."[11]

Peckham's theory applies in general terms to all fiction. But, as I have indicated, his model specifically fits the basic plot of cloistral fiction. And that plot is one way of indirectly describing the transaction between reader and writer. Seen from the outside, a reader bears considerable resemblance to those characters we have called receptors. He or she is sedentary or at least stationary; it really is difficult to read while you run. The reader looks passive, even lazy. Unless he is in a library, others seldom hesitate to interrupt since he does not seem to be doing anything. The reader is also a consumer. Whether or not he has bought the book, he is investing his time if not his money on its pages. And the reader resembles a host. By opening a book, he has invited an outsider, an alien consciousness, into his own. But, as we have already seen, the host-guest relationship is very close and often reversible. Hawthorne, for example, characteristically invites the reader into his abode, whether it be the Old Manse, the House of the Seven Gables, or the workshop of the artist. "Perhaps the reader, whom I cannot help considering as my guest in the Old Manse and entitled to all courtesy in the way of sight-showing,—perhaps he will choose to take a nearer view of the memorable spot."

The transaction between reader and storyteller is dramatized in Edward Albee's *The Zoo Story.* As the play opens, we see Peter, sedentary on a park bench, reading

[11]Ibid., pp. 271, 304-307.

a book. Jerry, the mobile stranger who invades Peter's privacy, later proves to be "'full of stories.'" Ordinarily, though, the connection between the plot and the reader-author relationship is less explicit. Very few of the receptors in our stories are actually readers. The closest would probably be the student in "The Raven" or the lawyer who reads Bartleby's legal documents. And very few of our mysterious strangers are actually writers. The big stranger in "The Man That Corrupted Hadleyburg" writes letters, Bartleby is a scrivener, and Alan Squier in *The Petrified Forest* is a failed novelist, but usually the intruders, as we have seen, have some other occupation or none at all.

Once the book has been opened and reading begins, the experience can no longer be effectively described from the outside. The receptive reader is involved in a transaction that is complicated and even mysterious. In the first place, the book itself, which had seemed static, is now kinetic—more like a mobile than an urn. And it virtually disappears as an object. "You are inside it; it is inside you; there is no longer either outside or inside."[12] Just how passive the reader is in this process depends not only on the character of author and reader but also on how closely we regard the experience. Sometimes it seems, as it did to Poe, that the reader of fiction is in the hands of a hypnotist or prestidigitator who makes the objects and routine of ordinary life disappear and replaces them with sights and sounds and smells from

[12]Georges Poulet, "Phenomenology of Reading," New Literary History 1 (1969): 54.

another world. Under the spell of few black marks on the page the reader is now being seduced or saved by a confidence man.

But "seduced or saved" wildly overstates the case. Fortunately readers do not uniformly succumb to the blandishments of advertising any more readily than they give in to the demands made upon them by James, Proust, or Faulkner. Yet during the reading experience itself, the reader surely plays a relatively passive role. Consider Poulet's minute examination of the "strange displacement of myself by the work:

> If the work thinks itself in me, does this mean that, during a complete loss of consciousness on my part, another thinking entity invades me, taking advantage of my unconsciousness in order to think itself without my being able to think it? Obviously not. The annexation of my consciousness by another (the other which is the work) in no way implies that I am the victim of any deprivation of consciousness. Everything happens, on the contrary, as though, from the moment I become a prey to what I read, I begin to share the use of my consciousness with this being whom I have tried to define and who is the conscious subject ensconced at the heart of the work. He and I, we start having a common consciousness. Doubtless, within this community of feeling, the parts played by each of us are not of equal importance. The consciousness inherent in the work is active and potent: it occupies the foreground; it is clearly related to its own world, to objects which are its objects. In opposition, I myself, although conscious of whatever it may be conscious of, I play a much more humble role, content to record passively all that is going in me. A lag takes place, a sort of schizoid distinction between what I feel and what the other feels; a confused awareness of delay, so that the work seems first to think by itself, and then to inform me what it has thought. Thus I often have the impression,

while reading, of simply witnessing an action which at the same time concerns and yet does not concern me. This provokes a certain feeling of surprise within me. I am a consciousness astonished by an existence which is not mine, but which I experience as though it were mine.[13]

Crucial parts of this description, we notice, resemble specifically the receptive consciousnesses of the lawyer in "Bartleby," Theodore Fischer in *The Mysterious Stranger,* Mr. Thompson in "Noon Wine," and Chief Bromden in *One Flew over the Cuckoo's Nest.* On the other hand, in stories like "The Gray Champion," "The Luck of Roaring Camp," and "The Killers," where the reader does not enter the receptor's mind, Poulet's description is too close-in to be relevant except in its description of the general effect of disorientation or displacement.

Another close-up view of the reading experience is the one offered by Stanley Fish. No one that I know of is more rigorously concerned with "an analysis of the developing responses of the reader as they succeed one another in time."[14] Instead of asking, as most of us customarily have done, what a given linguistic unit means, he asks what does this word, phrase, paragraph, chapter, poem, novel *do*? To use his simplest example, the two sentences, "He is sincere," and "Doubtless he is sincere," may, at a high level of generality, be said to have the same meaning. But this is misleading because it treats sentences as if they were containers from which a

[13]Ibid., pp. 59–60.

[14]Stanley E. Fish, "Literature in the Reader: Affective Stylistics," *New Literary History* 2 (1970): 126–27.

kernel of meaning is to be extracted. In the actual left-to-right temporal experience of reading, the beginning of the second sentence generates doubt in the very word "Doubtless" —an effect that partly undermines the affirmation of the unknown "he's" sincerity.

Although he starts with a simple question, Fish's analyses are elaborate and sensitive because he includes in his category of response "any and all of the activities provoked by a string of words"—not just a range of feelings but "the projection of syntactical and/or lexical probabilities; their subsequent occurrence or non-occurrence; attitudes toward persons, or things, or ideas referred to; to reversal or questioning of those attitudes; and much more." The "much more" includes "influences and pressures pre-dating the actual reading experience—questions of genre, history, etc."[15]

By concentrating on the interaction between an active mediating consciousness and the flow of words on the page, Fish is able to answer with considerable persuasiveness the hard questions asked at the beginning of this chapter. The reason we find both a measure of uniformity and yet considerable divergence in the interpretation of texts is that "most literary quarrels are not disagreements about response, but about a response to a response. What happens to one informed reader of a work will happen, within a range of nonessential variation, to another. It is only when readers become literary critics and the passing of judgment takes precedence over the reading experience, that opinions begin

[15]Ibid., p. 127.

to diverge."[16] Thus every reader of Faulkner will expose himself to his involutions, his confusions, interpolations, and delays; whether or not he likes or dislikes these devices or is ambivalent toward them, he will experience them.

Fish's method shows how the flow of language can both reassure and disorient the reader. But he is particularly adept at revealing the "progressive decertainizing" that occurs when we read some texts, and he is personally drawn to those works which provide unsettling literary experiences. Of the stories in our canon, I think he would prefer *The Confidence-Man*. Consider this description, related by a highly ambiguous narrator:

> Goneril was young, in person lithe and straight, too straight, indeed, for a woman, a complexion naturally rosy, and which would have been charmingly so, but for a certain hardness and bakedness, like that of the glazed colors on stone-ware. Her hair was of a deep, rich chestnut, but worn in close, short curls all round her head. Her Indian figure was not without its impairing effect on her bust, while her mouth would have been pretty but for a trace of moustache. Upon the whole, aided by the resources of the toilet, her appearance at distance was such, that some might have thought her, if anything, rather beautiful, though of a style of beauty rather peculiar and cactus-like.

If we ask, as Fish urges, what does this paragraph *do*? We must answer that it, like the whole book, gives us something and then takes it away. As informed readers we connect Melville's Goneril and Shakespeare's. Even

[16]Ibid., pp. 147–48.

though the allusion is sinister, we are reassured by our ability to make the connection. The series of direct affirmations ("Goneril was . . . Her hair was . . . Her Indian figure was . . .) is counterbalanced by a series of undermining qualifications and negations, just as the reader's progress through the paragraph is constantly slowed by comma pauses. Thus the final effect produced by the last sentence is one of tentative and distant affirmation dwindling off into unpleasant negation.

I am sure that Fish would have a great deal more to say about this paragraph if he wanted to. But his method, as he says, is not transferable; it is basically just a language-sensitizing device and, as such, extremely valuable. The chief weakness of his model of literary response, however, lies in his idealized conception of the reader. Who, after all, is "*the* reader"? In Fish's view he is the "informed reader," a competent speaker of the text's language who has full semantic knowledge of that language and literary competence. If we answer that the reader is really Stanley Fish, he would reply, "Yes and no." His responses as an actual reader are modified and made less idiosyncratic by his method. Better "to have an acknowledged and controlled subjectivity than objectivity [like that assumed by the New Critics] which is finally an illusion."[17]

Fish is probably right in his insistence that most of the disagreements over interpretation occur after we have completed the actual reading experience. But in spite of his candid analysis of the problem his version of the informed reader rigorously pursuing a left-to-right

[17]Ibid., pp. 145–46.

temporal perusal of the text remains somewhat idealized. This is where Norman Holland and his associates at the Buffalo Center for the Psychological Study of the Arts have a hard-earned advantage. They have been able to analyze closely what specific readers actually say about what they read. Fish would undoubtedly argue that they too are recording "a response to a response." But this postreading statement is, after all, what we must deal with in conversation, in the classroom, and in our own statements about our reading. "We can only understand what a particular reader has experienced *after* he has experienced and put forth his re-creation and synthesis beyond his own private mind."[18]

In three books and many gracefully composed essays Holland has outlined a general model of how we experience our world based upon specific analyses of how actual readers read. The basic principle in this model is not startling: "All of us, as we read, use the literary work to symbolize and finally to replicate ourselves." But with the help of such psychologists as Heinz Lichtenstein, Holland is able to describe this process with some degree of precision. To restate his basic principle: We experience the literary work within the medium of our "identity theme," a term referring to the "invariant that one can abstract from all of an individual's behavior including (or especially) his verbal behavior."[19] An individual lives out variations on an identity theme "much as a musician might play out an infinity of variations on a

[18]Holland, *5 Readers Reading*, p. 13.
[19]Ibid., p. 222.

single melody."[20] But it is we who abstract whatever it is that remains constant throughout a lifetime of variations. Of course, we can apply the same kind of scrutiny to our own behavior and come up with a version of our own identity theme.

By using Rorschach and TAT tests and by extensive informal interviews, Holland attempted to arrive at the identity themes of the five students whose responses are recorded and interpreted in *5 Readers Reading*. He found that, along with the first overarching principle—identity re-creates itself—there are three specific processes concurrently at work in the literary experience. First, the reader shapes the materials of the text into his own characteristic patterns of defense or adaptive strategies for coping with the world. Second, if he can make the work fit those strategies, he uses its elements to create fantasies and gratifications of the kinds that matter to him. And finally, he transforms those fantasies "toward a moral, esthetic, or intellectual 'point' that enables him to find in the work unity, significance, and pleasure."[21]

This is where Fish and Holland differ most sharply. To the question, When, in the analysis of a reading experience, does one come to the point? Fish answers: "'Never,' or, no sooner than the pressure to do so becomes unbearable (psychologically). . . . Coming to the point fulfills a need that most literature resists (if we

[20]"Unity Identity Text Self," *Publications of the Modern Language Association* 90 (October 1975): 816.

[21]Norman Holland, *Poems in Persons* (New York, 1973), p. 145.

open ourselves to it), the need to simplify and close. Coming to the point should be resisted."[22] Holland acknowledges the psychological need for coming to the point but denies that it should be resisted; for him the discovery of unity in a text or identity in selves is a way of achieving not only intellectual satisfaction but also deeply empathic relationship.[23]

The difference between Holland's later work and *The Dynamics of Literary Response* (1968) is minor but significant. He now emphasizes that stories

> do not "mean" in and of themselves. They do not fantasize or defend or adapt or transform. People do these things, using stories as the occasion (with more or less justification) for a certain theme, fantasy, or transformation. The problem then becomes understanding, not the story in formal isolation, but the story in relation to somebody's mind. Not a mind hypothesized, hypostatized, assumed, posited, or simply guessed at . . . we can only work with real minds in real people.[24]

With his training in both psychoanalysis and literary criticism Holland has been able to apply this method to a variety of materials, notably *Hamlet,* some modern short stories, and the lives and poetry of H. D. and Robert Frost. And by concentrating on the transaction between the self and the other within the principle of identity re-creation, Holland demolishes the old false barrier between subjectivity and objectivity, supplying us with a

[22]Fish, "Literature in the Reader," p. 148.
[23]Holland, "Unity Identity Text Self," p. 820.
[24]Holland, *5 Readers Reading,* p. 39.

paradigm that "applies not only to reading, but to a person's interaction with any external reality, human or non-human."[25]

Impressive as Holland's achievement is, we will find it more useful if we translate his terminology back into the dramatic metaphor. Our basic description of the literary experience will then read this way: Deprived of the existential immediacy of face-to-face oral communication, the writer fictionalizes the reader and the reader fictionalizes the writer, constructing from the text an identity that re-creates his own. As Walker Gibson and Father Ong have shown, the novelist, the advertiser, the historian, the scholar, and the simple letter writer all cast their readers in assigned roles. Thus Hemingway's reader assumes the part of a "companion-in-arms, somewhat later become confidant. It is a flattering role. Hemingway readers are encouraged to cultivate high self-esteem."[26]

As indicated above, the fictionalizing of the reader applies to all writing, not just fiction. But one of that form's fascinating aspects is that it explores, analogically at least, the reader's relation to the text. The reader's curiosity may be projected into the form of allowing him access to letters and journals. Or, as in "The Gold Bug," he may be invited to participate in breaking a secret code. Or his activity and unsettled role may be reflected

[25]Ibid., p. xiii; Norman Holland, "The New Paradigm," *New Literary History* 7 (Winter 1976): 339–45.

[26]Walker Gibson, *Tough, Sweet, and Stuffy* (Bloomington, Ind., 1966), pp. 3–33; Walter J. Ong, "The Writer's Audience Is Always a Fiction," *Publications of the Modern Language Association* 90 (January 1975): 13.

by the device of keeping the hero on the move. This active aspect of the reader must be one reason why fiction is so often referred to as an imaginary journey or quest.[27]

But if the quest is one of several analogies for the act of reading fiction, the intrusion is another. The writers of cloistral fiction have put into their narrative the process of incursion that happens whenever we perceive anything strange, whenever we perceive art, and more particularly whenever we perceive fiction. The author has denied any close connection between his personages and real people, living or dead. Who then is this voice who says, "They're out there," this fictional being who leaps from the page and eventually becomes better known to us than most of our friends in real life? And who is the ventriloquist behind this supposedly deaf-mute Indian? What ghastly being keeps repeating, "Nevermore," and what kind of person would contrive that refrain? What queer old bird would offer ancient Jewish wisdom to a modern family, and who would think of using that device?

In cloistral fiction the insiders "read" the stranger the way we size up any new acquaintance, studying his size, his facial expression, his clothes, his body language—in short, his "style." As the stranger in these stories communicates messages and cues to role playing to the insiders in a number of ways—by physical threat, by silence, by music, by a hypnotic refrain—so the insiders respond by guessing his identity. The situation is like taking a

[27]See, for example, Albert S. Cook, *The Meaning of Fiction* (Detroit, 1960), p. 243: "Any novel is a quest, sometimes even a Quest."

TAT test—writing a story in response to a picture. Or it is like that of chapter 2 in *The Confidence-Man*, where the deaf-mute writes messages on a slate and provokes widely varying responses as the insiders on this ship of fools try to place him and supply him with a "story": "Casper Hauser," "Green prophet from Utah," "Mooncalf," "Escaped convict, worn out from dodging."

So the reader fictionalizes the author. Cowed for years by fear of committing the "intentional fallacy," we tended to ignore the natural effort of all intense readers to identify the voice and character of the writer. As Melville said in his essay on Hawthorne's *Mosses from an Old Manse,* "No man can read a fine author, and relish him to his very bones, while he reads, without subsequently fancying to himself some ideal image of the man and his mind." Melville acknowledged in Hawthorne the gentle Indian-summer charm that others had perceived. But he identified with Hawthorne's "great power of blackness," just as he identified with "those short quick probings at the very axis of reality" that he wrote, were "the things that make Shakespeare Shakespeare."

It is sometimes said that Melville's essay tells us more about him than about Hawthorne. What it tells us about is the transaction between them; Melville's essay is a beautiful nineteenth-century exemplification of Holland's thesis. Themes, defenses, fantasies are in people, not in texts. As Melville said of Hawthorne to his readers: "Nor need you fix upon that blackness in him, if it suit you not. Nor, indeed, will all readers discern it, for it is, mostly, insinuated to those who may best understand it, and account for it."

Most of the best criticism of specific authors has been

written out of this kind of reading experience. One thinks of James's portrait of Hawthorne, D. H. Lawrence's *Studies in Classic American Literature*, Newton Arvin's *Melville,* Fiedler on Mark Twain, Allen Tate on Poe, and so on. All of these writings have strong "subjective biases," but they have been memorable and influential. It is also true that some of the worst literary criticism follows the same principle, some readers being so content or obsessed with their fictions that they prefer to ignore well-documented facts. Whitman has been cast in a number of ridiculous roles—a second Christ, a Marxist saint, a sex therapist. And the fictionalizing of Shakespeare as a Roman Catholic, an Anglican, a royalist, a democrat, and a homosexual ends, of course, in the recurring contention that Shakespeare himself is a fiction.[28] These absurdities confirm rather than deny Holland's basic premise—that each reader tries to construct from the elements of the work a match to his own characteristic style.

Is it possible, finally, to say anything significant about the interaction of readers and a whole set of works belonging to a genre or subgenre? Common observation would indicate a positive answer. Some readers devour detective stories; others prefer science fiction; still others are devoted to westerns. If we ask what readers respond to in cloistral fiction, our answers must be tentative and finally extensions of my own reactions. But I have discussed these stories with enough other readers

[28]See Leslie A. Fiedler, *An End to Innocence* (Boston, 1955), pp. 152–73. In part of this paragraph I am also indebted to an unpublished paper by David Russell.

to hazard some comments, even though I do not have the kinds of data used by Norman Holland.

Certain cloistral fictions, such as "Spotted Horses," "Cyclists' Raid," and *S.S. San Pedro,* appeal to the imagination of disaster. This powerful and primitive appeal is more spectacular in films, television programs, and plays than it is in print. Susan Sontag has observed that the science-fiction films of the 1950s, many of which follow the scenario of the mysterious intrusion, are not about science but are concerned "with the aesthetics of destruction, with the particular beauties to be found in wreaking havoc, making a mess."[29] The same point could be made about the technological Gothics, in which the invasion occurs on a subway or a huge jet plane; or the monster films, featuring gigantic insects and animals, growing clusters of various birds, or shapeless blobs. The lure of generalized disaster as a fantasy, Sontag remarks, is that it "releases one from normal obligations." (A tornado threatens on the horizon; it misses our town. Why do we feel disappointment along with relief? The feeling is irrational, but it is there).

The reader who tolerates and even enjoys being inside Chief Bromden's consciousness must experience his dislocations and hallucinations. Is the fog machine "out there" or in Broom's head? Do the walls of the asylum really contain intricate electronic devices? In differing degrees of intensity the same dissolution of distance between subject and object recurs in other stories. As we read James's "The Turn of the Screw," we cannot

[29]Susan Sontag, *Against Interpretation and Other Essays* (New York, 1966), p. 213.

be sure whether or not the governess is hallucinating the ghosts; in "Noon Wine" the murder of Mr. Hatch is presented to us in the thick August heat and through the distorted perception of Mr. Thompson; at the end of "Where Are You Going, Where Have You Been?" Connie regards herself as if she were an externally controlled object. In short, the reader of cloistral fiction is constantly aware of uncertainty bordering upon madness. The reader is in danger of being depersonalized, of being "taken over." But the experience is vicarious and protected. As the narrator of Carruth's *Appendix A* says, "You can shut me out any time you want to, just by closing the book."

This is really the only protection available to the reader of *The Confidence-Man,* which offers no relief from the process of "progressive decertainizing." But the reader of "Noon Wine" and "The Displaced Person" can find a subtler kind of reassurance from the stories themselves. In both stories our progressive incertitude is balanced by our growing confidence in the author's mastery of her craft.

"Noon Wine" is one of those minor masterpieces that can be read over and over again simply as a model of fictional technique. Mr. Thompson may be gradually losing control over his farm, but after a few paragraphs there is never any question in our minds about Miss Porter's control over her materials. The viewpoint shifts from close-up camera-eye observation to Mr. Thompson's consciousness, back out again, into Mrs. Thompson's dim vision, back out again, each transition handled with effortless grace. Early in the story Mr. Thompson's way of thinking about things is contemplated with detachment, permitting some wonderfully ironic touches:

> In spite of his situation in life, Mr. Thompson had never been able to outgrow his deep conviction that running a dairy and chasing after chickens was woman's work. . . . Slopping hogs was hired man's work, in Mr. Thompson's opinion. Killing hogs was a job for the boss, but scraping them and cutting them up was for the hired man again; and again woman's proper work was dressing meat, smoking, pickling, and making lard and sausage. . . . It was his dignity and his reputation that he cared about, and there were only a few kinds of work manly enough for Mr. Thompson to undertake with his own hands.

But by the end of the story the viewpoint has narrowed to Mr. Thompson's fumbling, desperate suicide—the only kind of work left that is manly enough for him to undertake with his own hands.

Miss Porter handles the passage of time with the same clean skill. Shifts in time, like shifts in perspective, are pegged to objects—the farm, the churn, the aging refrigerator—and, more important, they occur on a continuing flow of emotion. Although we look backward to the Thompsons' marriage and their murky problems in raising the children, the main movement of the story is relentlessly forward. The reader senses with grim foreboding that, for the moment Mr. Helton strides into the story as if "he knew where he was going,"every paragraph is headed toward the tragic conclusion.

Part of this effect is achieved through deftly ironic "pointers" or foreshadowing. But these devices are simply a small element in the total movement from disorder to order to disaster. More precisely, the story creates a sense of order successfully only insofar as it fully recognizes life's confusion: the Thompsons' bewildered awareness that both the farm and the children are getting out of hand, their difficulty in sustaining thought about anything important, their fumbling attempts at communication, and finally the inexplicable strangeness of human behavior. By the end of the story Thompson is in a situation parallel to Helton's at the beginning. A murderer, a stranger in his own neighborhood, he keeps playing *his* one tune over and over until he sees the hopelessness of his situation. As one sensitive reader has remarked, the song, "Noon Wine," that Helton plays over and over to himself metaphorically stands for "everything that people, in this story and out of it, cannot 'put into words, hardly into thoughts.'" In the end Thompson knows that it means "one man's being isolated with his understanding—the fateful privacy of meaning."[30]

As we read "Noon Wine," then, our fear that we are all dangerously close to breakdown is countered by our sense of the artist's control as we move to the fated end. A somewhat similar interaction between reader and author occurs in O'Connor's "The Displaced Person," now generally acknowledged as one of her most important stories.[31] But here we can be even more confident in our

[30]M. Wynn Thomas, "Strangers in a Strange Land: A Reading of 'Noon Wine,'" *American Literature* 47 (May 1975): 244.

[31]See especially Louis D. Rubin, Jr., "Flannery O'Connor: A Note on Literary Fashions," *Critique* 2 (Fall 1958): 11–18; Robert Fitzgerald, "The Countryside and the True Country," *Sewanee Review* 70 (Summer 1962): 380–94; and Sister M. Joselyn, "Thematic Centers

emphasis upon the author's craftsmanship because as academic critics we have knowledge of the changes she made in the text. For two versions of the story exist: the first published in the *Sewanee Review* in October, 1954, and the second published in *A Good Man Is Hard to Find* (1955) and since reprinted in other collections. [32] Incidentally, the fact that until recently no one seems to have noticed that the two versions radically differ tends to confirm O'Connor's statement about the oblivion of uncollected short stories: "One reason I like to publish short stories," she said, "is that nobody pays any attention to them. In ten years or so they begin to be known, but the process is not obnoxious. When you publish a novel, the racket is like a fox in a hen house."[33]

By comparing the two versions, we can learn quite a bit about O'Connor's art. Take the initial paragraph, for example:

1954 version:	1955 version:
Mrs. Shortley stood on a small prominence to the left of the pump house. Her folded arms were supported by a foundation of stomach from which the rest of her rose with the grand self-	The peacock was following Mrs. Shortley up the road to the hill where she meant to stand. Moving on behind the other, they looked like a complete procession. Her arms were folded and as she

in 'The Displaced Person," *Studies in Short Fiction* 1 (Winter 1964): 84–92.

[32]See Roy R. Male, "The Two Versions of 'The Displaced Person,' " *Studies in Short Fiction* 7 (Summer 1970): 457. Much of that article is reprinted here.

[33]*The Added Dimension: The Art and Mind of Flannery O'Connor,* ed. Melvin J. Friedman and Lewis A. Lawson (New York, 1966), p. 253.

confidence of a mountain, up narrowing bulges of granite to two icy blue points of light, that surveyed the surrounding territory. It was the kind of stomach that the faces of Washington, Jefferson, and Lee might have been carved on, or a sign splashed that said, DAMNNATION TO THE EVIL-DOER. YOU WILL BE UNCOVERED.

mounted the prominence, she might have been the giant wife of the countryside, come out at some sign of danger to see what the trouble was. She stood on two tremendous legs, with the grand self-confidence of a mountain, and rose, up narrowing bulges of granite, to two icy blue points of light that pierced forward, surveying everything. She ignored the white afternoon sun which was creeping behind a ragged wall of cloud as if it pretended to be an intruder and cast her gaze down the red clay road that turned off from the highway.

In the 1955 version the neutral detail of the pump house has been replaced by the peacock, which will assume a major symbolic role in the story, and the first two sentences now provide movement to balance the essentially static description of Mrs. Shortley. The revised ending of the first sentence—"where she meant to stand"—ties in with the new foreshadowing and the new suggestion that she resembles "the giant wife of the countryside" to extend the dimensions of the story. Grotesque and mean as she is, Mrs. Shortley nevertheless bears a generic resemblance to some of our other receptors: she will stand firm, "come out at some sign of danger," and resist the intruder.

O'Connor once said that "sometimes you need time

between you and the story before you can really see it whole," and that seems to have been what happened here. The first version of the story is really a fragment; it ends with the displacement and death of Mrs. Shortley. This is only part 1 of the revised version, which rigorously pushes the process of displacement until its widening circle includes all the characters. The reader is meant to infer, as Robert Fitzgerald did in 1962, that this is a "tale of the displacement of persons, or, better, of the human Person displaced."[34]

As I noted earlier (chapter 2), for displacement to have its full dramatic effect the importance of "place"—not only location but class distinctions, manners, and vocation—must be established. As a nonexperimental but modern writer, O'Connor renders these values concretely by refracting them through the viewpoint first of Mrs. Shortley and then of Mrs. McIntyre. The initial technical question is when to move in to take Mrs. Shortley's point of view. "Never go inside a character's head until you know what he looks like," O'Connor told a group of young writers.[35] In the 1954 version she describes Mrs. Shortley's clothing and the local topography, and seems somewhat hesitant to move in:

> She had on a pair of red rubber boots spattered with clay, and a blue and yellow flowered dress that had once been four chicken feed sacks. From her elevation she could see the road that ran from the highway to the big house and down to the barn and over to her own house and then disappeared in a

[34]Fitzgerald, "The Countryside and the True Country," p. 393.
[35]Friedman, *The Added Dimension,* p. 250.

fold between two pastures. Turning in from the highway was a black car.

Across the road from her, over by the tool shed, the two negroes, Astor and Sulk, had stopped work to watch. They were hidden by a fig tree but she knew they were there. Mrs. McIntyre came down the front steps of the big house just as the black car stopped at the walk. She had on a giant-size smile as if, since these people couldn't talk, you had to enlarge the look on your face to make them understand how you felt. "That there's her welcome look," Mrs. Shortley muttered, and very slowly she turned up her own mouth to imitate it and stood there smiling icily for almost a minute. Then the smile vanished and her usual look of omniscience returned.

The reference to the way Mrs. McIntyre felt blurs the point of view, and the ending of the paragraph leaves us still outside Mrs. Shortley. And a minor point: To have Astor and Sulk "hidden by a fig tree" may provoke the wrong kind of allegorical associations. In the revision, satisfied that she knows, Mrs. Shortley's appearance and location, the author reduces the distance between herself and her character, moves in much more surely and economically.

Mrs. Shortley was watching a black car turn through the gate from the highway. Over by the tool shed, about fifteen feet away, the two Negroes, Astor and Sulk, had stopped work to watch. They were hidden by a mulberry tree but Mrs. Shortley knew they were there.

Mrs. McIntyre was coming down the steps of her house to meet the car. She had on her largest smile but Mrs. Shortley, even from her distance, could detect a nervous slide in it. These people who were coming were only hired help, like the Shortleys themselves or the Negroes. Yet here was the owner of the place out to welcome them. Here she was, wearing her best clothes and a string of beads, and now bounding forward with her mouth stretched.

The focus has sharpened. Mrs. Shortley is the observer, Mrs. McIntyre and the intruding strangers the things observed. So that there will be no doubt on this point, Miss O'Connor begins succeeding paragraphs of the revised version with further cues: "Mrs. Shortley's vision narrowed . . . and then widened. . . . She looked closer, squinting." Taken out of context, these aids to the reader's perspective seem rather obvious, but point of view, especially at the beginning of a story, is nothing to be timid about. "Don't be subtle until the fourth page," was another of the author's tips to beginners.[36]

References to the angle of vision are empty, of course, unless there is increased concreteness in the things observed. In the first version the description of the intruders as they tamely emerged from the car was toneless and vague: "The first one to get out of the car was the priest, a long-legged black figure with a white hat on. He opened the back door and out came two children, a boy and a girl, and then a woman. Out of the front door came the man." In the revision the idiom is closer to Mrs. Shortley's, the verbs become more active, and the intruders, especially the Displaced Person, assume definite shapes.

The car stopped at the walk just as she did and the priest was the first to get out. He was a long-legged black-suited old man with a white hat on and a collar that he wore backwards, which, Mrs. Shortley knew, was what priests did who wanted

[36]Ibid., p. 251.

to be known as priests. It was this priest who had arranged for these people to come here. He opened the back door of the car and out jumped two children, a boy and a girl, and then, stepping more slowly, a woman in brown, shaped like a peanut. Then the front door opened and out stepped the man, the Displaced Person. He was short and a little sway-backed and wore gold-rimmed spectacles.

The first real sign that the Displaced Person will become the Displacer comes when he kisses Mrs. McIntyre's hand. This alien gesture, added in the revision, makes an indelible impression upon Mrs. Shortley. It presages the whole nightmare of intrusion that slowly seeps into her mind: the invasion of a foreign language—"The Polish words and the English words coming at each other, stalking forward, not sentences, just words, gabble, gabble, gabble"—uttered by people with alien names, Gobblehooks or Guizacs, diabolical people with an unreformed religion, whose end would be the dissolution of all social and racial distinctions.

If foreign hired help can kiss the hand of the lady who hires and fires, then the whole system, as Mrs. Shortley has known it and as O'Connor acutely portrays it, is threatened. It is an order of tacitly acknowledged privacies and inadequacies. Everybody knows but nobody mentions the fact that the Negroes steal; Mr. Shortley smokes in the barn, but Mrs. McIntyre complains about it only to his wife; both the Negroes and Mr. Shortley run stills without interference from each other or their employer. But now, Mrs. Shortley observes, "with foreigners on the place, with people who were all eyes and no understanding, who had come from a place continually fighting, where the religion had not been reformed—with this kind of people, you had to be on the lookout every minute."

This fear of total displacement is the meaning of the grotesque newsreel vision, carried over without change from the first version, which I would guess to have been the germ of the story. Deeply imbedded in Mrs. Shortley's memory, it shows "naked people all in a heap, their arms and legs tangled together, a head thrust in here, a head there, a foot, a knee, a part that should have been covered up sticking out, a hand raised clutching nothing. Before you could realize that it was real and take it into your head, the picture changed and a hollow-sounding voice was saying, "Time marches on." In Flannery O'Connor's last published story, "Revelation," a very similar vision comes to Mrs. Turpin, and it comes, significantly, after her traditional analysis of classes in the South has broken down when confronted with social change.

The grisly image first seen in the newsreel recurs when Mrs. Shortley responds to the mystical command to prophesy. "'The children of wicked nations will be butchered,' she said in a loud voice. 'Legs where arms should be, foot to face, ear in the palm of hand. Who will remain whole? Who?'" And it is repeated at the end of part 1 as the Shortley family is being displaced. They are riding off in the crammed car, the children asking in higher and higher voices, "'Where we goin, Ma? Where we goin?'" and Mrs. Shortley, as she dies, is "clutching at everything she could put her hands on and hugging it to herself, Mr. Shortley's head, Sarah Mae's leg, . . . her own big moon-like knee." The process begun when Mr. Guizac kissed his employer's hand concludes for Mrs.

Shortley as she seems to "contemplate for the first time the tremendous frontiers of her true country."

This, as I have said, is where the first version ends. The remainder of the story, in which Mrs. McIntyre replaces Mrs. Shortley as point-of-view character and wife of the countryside, has been prepared for by small but significant changes in part 1. O'Connor fills in part of Mrs. McIntyre's past and changes her age from fifty to sixty. This makes her failing health at the end more credible and adds depth to her reminiscences as she and the oldest Negro politely instruct each other on the meaning of the farm's history. Their refrain—"'We've seen them come and seen them go'"—reminds us that a stream of individuals has slowly flowed through the domestic hierarchy. For the most part its essential structure has remained unchanged, though tractors have displaced mules. From Mrs. McIntyre's perspective the process has been one long overflow. Husbands have come and gone; so have the white trash, tenant farmers, and dairymen, each of them stealing a little on the way (O'Connor even extends the imagery of drainage to her description of Mr. Shortley's face, which is "sharply rutted" with a "washout under each cheek and two long crevices eaten down both sides of his blistered mouth"). Mean, devoted to money, Mrs. McIntyre has, nevertheless, some of the stature that comes from sheer tough endurance. She has survived "the constant drain of a tribe of moody unpredictable Negroes" and has even held her own "against the incidental bloodsuckers, the cattle dealers and the lumber men and the buyers and sellers of anything who drove up in pieced-together trucks and honked in the yard." And with the arrival of the mechanically efficient Pole, she feels that at last she has someone she can depend on. "He was kind of a miracle that she had seen happen and that she talked about but that she still didn't believe."

In the revision of part 1, O'Connor added one other point, essential in foreshadowing the dénouement of the story. This was the secret, confided to Mr. Shortley by his wife before her death, that the Pole was planning to arrange a marriage between the young Negro, Sulk, and Mr. Guizac's sixteen-year-old blond cousin. Mrs. McIntyre's discovery of this plot changes her whole perspective. Her Polish savior becomes the destroyer, a mechanical monster whose eyes "were like two bright nails behind his goldrimmed spectacles that had been mended over the nose with haywire." From this point on, it is simply a matter of time before the "terrible accident" predicted by Mrs. Shortley, set in motion by Mr. Shortley, and collaborated in by Sulk and Mrs. McIntyre occurs, and everyone except the priest and the peacock is displaced.

A final, or nearly final, word about the peacock. Writers participating in panel discussions are always asked questions, usually inane, about symbolism in their work. A familiar way out is to recite Mary McCarthy's anecdote about the student in a writing class who, after being mildly praised by McCarthy for her story, replied: "But my teacher read this and said, 'Well, all right, but now we have to go back and put in the symbols.'" A polite laugh ensues, the questioner is properly squelched, and the panelists can go on to something more interesting. This, in fact, is what happened when

Katherine Anne Porter told the McCarthy anecdote during a panel discussion with O'Connor and others at Wesleyan College in Macon, Georgia, in 1960.[37] Yet in rewriting "The Displaced Person," the author did go back and put in one of the major symbols, the peacock.

What counts, of course, is not when but how she put the symbol in. It appears in the first two paragraphs, recurs at frequent intervals, and is prominent in the ending, when the bird is fed by the priest before he explains the doctrines of the church to the failing Mrs. McIntyre. The priest, the peacock, and the Displaced Person combine to give the story the added religious dimension that is O'Connor's trademark. "Combine" is too weak a word. The religious and secular worlds are jammed together in a series of telling scenes where the cross-talk asks, in effect, what would happen if, without losing the concreteness of the known world, we took the Bible seriously. The best example occurs when the peacock spreads his tail and the priest says, "'Christ will come like that!'"

> Mrs. McIntyre's face assumed a set puritanical expression and she reddened. Christ in the conversation embarassed her the way sex had her mother. "It is not my responsibility that Mr. Guizac has nowhere to go," she said. "I don't find myself responsible for all the extra people in the world."
>
> The old man didn't seem to hear her. His attention was fixed on the cock who was taking minute steps backward, his head against the spread tail.
>
> "The Transfiguration," he murmured.

[37] *Recent Southern Fiction: A Panel Discussion* (Macon, Ga., 1960), p. 12.

She had no idea what he was talking about. "Mr. Guizac didn't have to come here in the first place," she said, giving him a hard look.

The cock lowered his tail and began to pick grass.

"He didn't have to come in the first place," she repeated, emphasizing each word.

The old man smiled absently. "He came to redeem us," he said, and blandly reached for her hand and shook it and said he must go.

O'Connor is concerned with showing us that human beings are valuable and responsible. This, I take it, is what the Redemption means. But she is more pointedly showing us that their value does not lie in their charm. She wants to remind her readers of what is very easy for modern Christians to forget: that Christ came not for the glorification of the good but to bring sinners like Mrs. McIntyre to redemption. Yet, as her rather unsympathetic portrayal of the priest indicates, she reveals this within the limits of her art.

Although she went back and put in the symbol, one can appreciate the writer's irritation with the now obviously sterile practice of running all fiction through the image-symbol-theme grid. As O'Connor said during the panel discussion at Wesleyan College, "So many students approach a story as if it were a problem in algebra: find *X* and when they find *X* they can dismiss the rest of it." The peacock in this story means different things to different characters. It is "nothing but a peachicken" to Mrs. Shortley, "another mouth to feed" to Mrs. McIntyre, a symbol of Christ to the priest. But its essence, at last, is mystery, and the mystery should be allowed to remain.

But even if our interpretation allows the mystery to remain and thus avoids the stigma of being rigid or mathematical, it still retains its emphasis on technique. As a white, northern, male, academic critic, I counter the general fear of displacement aroused in me by the story with my intellectual pleasure in discovering its formal control.

A different example of the way a writer fictionalizes the reader and the reader fictionalizes the writer can be found in an article appropriately entitled "Beyond the Peacock: The Reconstruction of Flannery O'Connor." It is by Alice Walker, the black novelist who as a child lived within a few miles of Flannery O'Connor's home. Twenty years younger than O'Connor, Alice Walker read her books "endlessly" when she was in college, "Scarcely aware of the difference between her racial and economic background and my own." Then, after a period of angry reaction in which she sought and found black writers and ignored white ones, Walker concluded that she would "never be satisfied with a segregated literature. I would have to read Zora Hurston *and* Flannery O'Connor, Nella Larsen *and* Carson McCullers, Jean Toomer *and* William Faulkner, before I could begin to feel *well* read at all."

There is some acute literary criticism in this article: direct, lucid comments on O'Connor's demythifying of southern settings and characters ("not a whiff of magnolia . . . in the air"), her ironic humor, her handling of religious themes ("no religious tracts, nothing haloed softly in celestial light, not even any happy endings"). "To O'Connor, in fact, Jesus was God, and he won only by losing. She perceived that not much has been learned by his death by crucifixion, and that it is only by his continual, repeated dying—touching one's own life in a direct searing way—that the meaning of that original loss is pressed into the heart of the individual."

But the literary criticism is interwoven with Walker's account of a trip she made back to Georgia in 1974. With her mother she went to see two houses—her own and O'Connor's—to see "at the very least, whether her peacocks would be still around." At the most, her trip south was, as she told her mother, an effort to find a "wholeness." To her mother's comment, "'You look whole enough to me,'" Alice Walker answered: "'No . . . because everything around me is split up, deliberately split up. History split up. Literature split up, and people are split up too. It makes people do ignorant things.'" She was talking primarily about racial separatism but also about writing and the relation between them: "Each writer writes the missing parts to the other writer's story. And the whole story is what I'm after.'"

The description of her visit to the two houses—hers an abandoned share-farmer shack, formerly subject to the trespass of the crooked landlord; Flannery O'Connor's a vacant but neatly kept white house, formerly subject to the intrusion of lupus—is written out of rage and understanding. She knocks at the door of the O'Connor house. "It is not an entirely empty or symbolic gesture: I have come to this vacant house to learn about myself in relation to Flannery O'Connor, and will learn it whether anyone is at home or not." At this moment she is overcome by fury: "fury that someone is paid to take care of her house, though no one lives in it, and that her house still, in fact, stands, while mine—

which of course we never owned anyway—is slowly rotting into dust. Her house becomes—in an instant—the symbol of my own disinheritance, and for that instant I hate her guts. All that she has meant to me is diminished, though her diminishment within me is against my will."

It is bitterness so deep that it amounts to a yearning for revolution. Walker muses that "it all comes back to houses. To how people live. There are people who own houses to live in and poor people who do not. And this is wrong. . . . I think: I would level this country with the sweep of my hand, if I could." Yet as she and her mother walk about the yard, listening to the soft rustle of the peacock's tails, she notices how completely O'Connor had described her limited world in her fiction. "I remind myself of her courage and of how much—in her art—she has helped me to see. She destroyed the last vestiges of sentimentality in white Southern writing; she caused white women to look ridiculous on pedestals, and she approached her black characters—as a mature artist—with unusual humility and restraint. She also cast spells and worked magic with the written word. The magic, the wit, and the mystery of Flannery O'Connor I know I will always love."[38]

Perhaps only writers respond to other writers this intensely. Yet for some readers Alice Walker's experience, though unique in its particulars, is representative. We are at once disturbed and comforted to realize that amid the other strangely familiar objects that violate and

[38]Alice Walker, "Beyond the Peacock: The Reconstruction of Flannery O'Connor," *Ms.* 4 (December, 1975): 77–106.

tranquilize our domestic lives—the jangling but reassuring telephone, the lull and cacophony of the stereo, the numbing, relentlessly consumptive, but occasionally eye-opening television set—there remain some books, some authors, whose words at first directly trespass upon our consciousness but when seen in retrospect become like old friends, even though the magic, the wit, and the mystery remain.

Thus in its quiet way the act of reading contains the larger rhythms of going out and taking in that constitute our experience. I noted earlier that, on the most elemental level, long novels have been characterized as quests, journeys from the familiar to the strange, mirrors carried down a road. But we have seen that a very considerable number of shorter fictions in this country (and elsewhere) present us with the intrusion of the strange upon the familiar. Fresh from discussing Flannery O'Connor's Christ-haunted South, I found it ironically appropriate in 1977 that a man from rural Georgia should invade the White House. Jimmy Carter's election, as he tirelessly reminded us, came from a series of long journeys all over the country. But for the natives of official Washington, a place constantly under criticism as a sequestered bureaucracy cut off from the people, his inauguration was cloistral fiction come to life. Editorial writers asked, "Who is this stranger?" and "Who will have the power?" Here was a man whose initials were J. C., saying, "Trust me." In his past and beneath his smile were suggestions of steel-hard technological efficiency. What remained in doubt was the possible transformation. Would the Tyrants Within be displaced, the power of inertia, cynicism, and greed exorcised, the Giant Inflation conquered? Probably not—or at any rate the answers would not be clear. Political life goes on interminably; our fictions, even those that seem open-ended, mercifully come to a close.

Appendix

Representative Cloistral Fictions (Mostly American)

Albee, Edward: *The Zoo Story*
Balzac, Honoré de: "Christ in Flanders"
Beckett, Samuel: *Waiting for Godot*
Benét, Stephen Vincent: "The Devil and Daniel Webster"
Bethune, Lebert: "The Burglar"
Conrad, Joseph: *The Nigger of the Narcissus,* "The Secret Sharer"
Cozzens, James Gould: *Castaway, S.S. San Pedro*
Crane, Stephen: "The Blue Hotel"
Dickens, Charles: "A Christmas Carol," "The Haunted Man"
Doctorow, E. L.: *Welcome to Hard Times*
Faulkner, William: "Spotted Horses"
Hardy, Thomas: "The Three Strangers," "The Fiddler of the Reels"
Harte, Bret: "The Luck of Roaring Camp"
Hawthorne, Nathaniel: "The Gray Champion," "The Ambitious Guest"

Hemingway, Ernest: "The Killers," "The Snows of Kilimanjaro"
Howells, William Dean: *A Traveller from Altruria*
Irving, Washington: "The Little Man in Black," "The Stout Gentleman"
James, Henry: "The Jolly Corner," "The Turn of the Screw"
Kesey, Ken: *One Flew over the Cuckoo's Nest*
McCullers, Carson: "The Ballad of the Sad Café"
Malamud, Bernard: "The Jewbird"
Maupassant, Guy de: "The Horla"
Melville, Herman: "Bartleby the Scrivener," "The Lightning-Rod Man" *The Confidence–Man*
Miller, Arthur: *A View from the Bridge*
Oates, Joyce Carol: "Where Are You Going, Where Have You Been?"
O'Brien, Fitz-James: "What Was It?"
O'Connor, Flannery: "A Circle in the Fire," "Good Country People," "The Life You Save May Be Your Own," "The Displaced Person"
Poe, Edgar Allan: "The Masque of the Red Death," "The Angel of the Odd," "Mystification," "The Raven," "The Sphinx," "The Devil in the Belfry," "The Duc de l'Omelette"
Porter, Katherine Anne: "Noon Wine"
Robinson, Edwin A.: "Flammonde"
Rooney, Frank: "Cyclists' Raid"
Sherwood, Robert E.: *The Petrified Forest*
Singer, Isaac B.: "Old Love"
Spark, Muriel: *Memento Mori*
Steinbeck, John: "The Chrysanthemums"

Twain, Mark: "The Man That Corrupted Hadleyburg,"
The Mysterious Stranger
Updike, John: "Nakedness"
Warren, Robert Penn: "Blackberry Winter"

Index